Pack Prints

ENG 1003: COMPOSITION I

Campus Writing Program • Second Edition
Department of English, Philosophy, and World Languages .
Arkansas State University

Editor-in-Chief
Kristi Murray Costello

Assistant Editors
Airek Beauchamp • Kerri L. Bennett

Narrative Genre Editor
Kristi Murray Costello

Rhetorical Analysis Genre Editors
Tabatha Simpson-Farrow • Mitchell Wells

Argument Genre Editor
Kerri L. Bennett

Argument Genre Assistant Editors
Leslie Reed • Jonathan Carmack

Cover Artist
Ross Carroll

Layout Design Editors
John Abernathy • Kerri L. Bennett

macmillan learning
curriculum solutions

Printed in the United States of America

10 9 8 7 6 5 4 3 2 1

ISBN 978-0-7380-9282-9

Macmillan Learning Curriculum Solutions
14903 Pilot Drive
Plymouth, MI 48170
www.macmillanlearning.com

Costello 9282-9 F17

macmillan learning
curriculum solutions

Sustainability
Hayden-McNeil's standard paper stock uses a minimum of 30% post-consumer waste. We offer higher % options by request, including a 100% recycled stock. Additionally, Hayden-McNeil Custom Digital provides authors with the opportunity to convert print products to a digital format. Hayden-McNeil is part of a larger sustainability initiative through Macmillan Learning. Visit http://sustainability.macmillan.com to learn more.

bedford/st. martin's • hayden-mcneil
w.h. freeman • worth publishers

Pack Prints Staff

Editor-in-Chief
Kristi Murray Costello

Assistant Editors
Airek Beauchamp • Kerri L. Bennett

Narrative Genre Editor
Kristi Murray Costello

Rhetorical Analysis Genre Editors
Tabatha Simpson-Farrow • Mitchell Wells

Argument Genre Editor
Kerri L. Bennett

Argument Genre Assistant Editors
Leslie Reed • Jonathan Carmack

Cover Artist
Ross Carroll

Layout Design Editors
John Abernathy • Kerri L. Bennett

Editorial Staff
Helen Duclos

Roy Tanksley

Marie-Jose Patton

Elizabeth Chamberlain

Audrey Belton

McKenzie Cagle Fair

Robyn Frost

Tianna Baker

Robin Everett

John Abernathy

Bethany Gallimore

Rae Summers-Thompson

Faculty Authors
Robert Robinette

Carmen Lanos Williams

Kristi Murray Costello

Marie-Jose Patton

Elizabeth Chamberlain

Leslie Reed

Mitchell Wells

Tabatha Simpson-Farrow

Student Authors

Lathan Garnett	"Tear-Stained Pages"
Tyler Graham	"The Thunder Never Ends"
Amanda Cunningham	"Can You Hear Me?"
Ashlyn Orewiler	"Pickup Parasailing"
Bethany Gallimore	"A Future So Bright" and "Our Planet, Our Plastic, and Our Problem"
Landon Grimmett	"The House Always Wins: An Analysis of a Fundamentalist Tradition in a Community"
Caroline Pulliam	"The Law of Human Nature"
Mazie Tackett	"UNITED States of America"
Corbin Edwards	"A Benchmark in Hip Hop"
Mohammed Ghias	"Samsung Galaxy S6 Plays It Smart" and "Monstrosity"
Connor Patrom	"To Vote or Not to Vote"
Brittney Nicole Smith	"Airline High School vs. ACLU"
Samuel Vickers	"Cries Heard around the World"
Amber Hatcher	"Muggles and Mudbloods and Creatures, Oh My! Racism in the Wizarding World"
William Kazyak	"Deception and Destruction: Operation Fortitude and the Allied Aerial Support for Operation Overlord"
Courtney Baker	"Coal Mining: From Providing to Destroying"

Table of Contents

Pack Prints

Table of Contents

Acknowledgements

I would like to recognize all of the people who made this text possible. Of course, this begins with the Arkansas State University student writers who are generously sharing their work with us, but it extends to many others.

I appreciate the instructors of the students who have been included in this text for not only providing quality instruction to our students, but also for encouraging their students to submit their great work. The Composition instructors of the authors of this edition of Pack Prints are Kerri Bennett, Robin Everett, Marcus Tribbett, Tabatha Simpson-Farrow, Mark Towell, Brandy Humphrey, Leslie Reed, Mitch Wells, Glinda Hall, Geoffrey Clegg, and Haley Fitzgerald. Without the great teaching of great faculty, we would not have the great essays that comprise this book.

I would also like to extend thanks to the *Pack Prints* Editorial Board not just for reading student essays and making the difficult decisions as to which few essays, out of the hundreds submitted, should be published, but also for being open to and supporting this new campus tradition: Tianna Baker, Marie-Jose Patton, Bethany Gallimore, Robyn Frost, Robin Everett, John Abernathy, Helen Duclos, Roy Tanksley, Elizabeth Chamberlain, Rae Summers-Thompson, McKenzie Cagle Fair, and Audrey Belton. I am also very grateful to: Layout Editors, Kerri Bennett and John Abernathy; Cover Artist, Ross Carroll; Assistant Genre Editors, Leslie Reed and Jonathan Carmack; Genre Editors, Mitchell Wells and Tabatha Simpson; and Assistant Editors, Airek Beauchamp and Kerri Bennett. Without their efforts, professionalism, dedication, and support throughout this project, you would not have this book in front of you.

Dr. Mike Hogan and Dr. Kelly Kinney are also recipients of my sincerest gratitude. Hogan's *Beyond the Blank Page*, Kinney's *Binghamton Writes*, and the inspiring, educational experiences I had working on both of these student anthologies provided me with the expertise and confidence needed to move forward with the first and subsequent editions of *Pack Prints*.

This text would not have been possible without the guidance, support, flexibility, and expertise of Lisa Wess, Douglas Dentino, and their colleagues at Hayden-McNeil. As has always been my experience with Hayden-McNeil, they worked diligently and efficiently on this project. Likewise, neither this text nor any of the steps the Writing Program has taken this year could have been possible without the unwavering support of the College of Liberal Arts and Communication, specifically Dean Carl Cates and Associate Dean Deborah Chappel-Traylor. Not only would this book not exist, but I wouldn't be who I am or where I am without the friendship and encouragement of Department Chair of the Department of English, Philosophy, and World Languages, Janelle Collins, or the big ideas, follow-through, and camaraderie of my dear friend and colleague, Airek Beauchamp. Thank you to my friends, Lisa and Tim Bohn, Sarah Scott, Carmen Williams, and Kendra Eads for instinctively knowing when to listen and when to make me laugh—and you are so good at both. As always, I am grateful to my brilliant husband and best friend, Liam Costello, for his love, input, help, and reassurances, particularly in times of stress. In return for all of your awesomeness, I promise not to take on another book for at least two years.

Lastly, I would like to extend my thanks to you, the reader, for being part of our tradition of celebrating students' writing. In reading this edition of *Pack Prints*, you are supporting Arkansas State University's Campus Writing Program, which includes a lovely and impressive group of faculty, students, and administrators. To further support the Arkansas State University Writing Program and Arkansas State University writers, be sure to submit or encourage your students to submit great essays for the next edition!

Dr. Kristi Costello

Editor-in-Chief, Pack Prints

Director, Writing Program and Writing Center

Assistant Professor, Rhetoric, Composition, and Writing Studies

A Note to Readers

What you have in front of you is the second edition, of what we hope will be many editions, of *Pack Prints*, Arkansas State University's anthology of exemplar student writing. With the exception of the section introductions, citation guides, assignment prompts, and the section on library and Information Research, which were written by faculty, the writing in this book is that of Arkansas State University students. As you will learn from reading this text, Arkansas State University students are bright and adventurous, and we, the faculty at Arkansas State University, love working with them. In addition to showing off our students' impressive writing, our hope is that *Pack Prints* will facilitate learning for Arkansas State University students and teaching for Arkansas State University faculty.

This text has been broken into five sections: Narrative, Analysis, Argument, Additional Resources, and a Style Guide complete with information regarding and student examples formatted in MLA, Chicago (CMS), and APA style. The included genres, narrative, analysis, and argument, are all genres in which students will engage in their Composition I course. However, you will see, as you read through each section, that students' essays, though of the same genre, are very different. For example, the Narrative section includes the subgenres of memoirs, literacy narratives, and personal essays. In the Analysis section, some of the essays are rhetorical analyses, while others are literary analyses or process analyses. In the Argument section, you'll find position papers, op-eds, extended definition essays, and argumentative essays. You'll notice that some of the writers' voices are informal and conversational, while others are academic and formal. In general, throughout the text, if you look closely, you will also see that some students use primary and secondary sources to substantiate their claims, while others' claims are evidenced by their personal experiences. These differences in content, organization, and style illustrate how different writing occasions call for different conventions. We encourage you to consider and discuss these rhetorical and stylistic conventions and differences as you work your way through the text and the course. Doing so will help facilitate the process of considering how, when, and why to apply these conventions and others to your own writing.

Please note that all of the essays published in this text have undergone revision, some of them, extensively so. In fact, as you read through the student authors' biographies, you will see that many of them discuss the revision process. While some authors, like Tyler Graham and Lathan Garnett, discuss how quickly and easily they wrote the first drafts of their essays, others, like Courtney Baker and Bethany Gallimore, acknowledge revision as difficult and sometimes tedious, but ultimately worth it. Thus, students should not be intimidated by the essays in this text; instead, we hope you will see that through hard work and revision you too can create polished, publishable writing. Instructors, students, and other readers should also note that while the essays in this anthology are of high quality, they are not perfect nor above criticism. The works contained in this text should provide models, not just for imitation, but also for discussion and critique. While we ask that instructors and students treat all of the students' work with respect, we urge classes to re-envision the pieces, hypothesizing how these works could be even better and what they would have done differently were the pieces their own.

In the end, we hope you enjoy reading this text as much as we enjoyed writing and editing it!

Kristi Costello, Editor-In-Chief

A User's Guide to *Pack Prints*: Composition and Rhetorical Genre Studies

A User's Guide to *Pack Prints*: Composition and Rhetorical Genre Studies

Kristi Murray Costello

Composition I (ENG1003) provides Arkansas State University students "study and practice of fundamentals of written communication including principles of grammar, punctuation, spelling, organization, and careful analytical reading" (*2014–2015 Undergraduate Bulletin* 468). Composition II (ENG1013) "continues the practice of ENG 1003, to develop further the skills learned in that course. Based on reading and discussion of various types of writing, the students' essays will provide practice in different kinds of rhetorical development including research and documentation" (*2014–2015 Undergraduate Bulletin* 468). Put shortly, while Composition I is where students practice writing, develop their writing processes, begin to think of themselves as writers, and learn to make the moves successful writers make, Composition II is where students learn and practice academic writing strategies and techniques, begin to think of themselves as *scholars*, and learn to make the moves successful scholars make. What they share is that both courses are designed to help students become stronger writers and critical thinkers. To this end, both courses are based on a Rhetorical Genre Studies Model and thus require students to write, read, analyze, and critique different genres.

WHAT ARE GENRES?

Richard Johnson-Sheehan and Charles Paine explain in *Writing Today* that "genres are ways of writing and speaking that help people communicate and work together in specific situations" (7). Understanding and applying knowledge of genres to your writing can help you write rhetorically (effective and persuasive). In fact, Amy J. Devitt artfully explains in "Genre Pedagogies" how "genres make rhetoric visible," meaning that understanding genres enables us to recognize effective writing. Effective writing in one genre may look very different from effective writing in another genre. Let's think about Tweets, for example. Twitter defines a Tweet as "an expression of a moment or idea shared on Twitter that can contain, text, photos, and videos" (Twitter).

The Genre of the Tweet

Though Twitter has only been available since 2006, it has 313 million active users and a simple Google search on how to Tweet yields nearly a billion results (Twitter). These results range from blogs that contain anecdotal advice about what to Tweet and what not to Tweet to Buzzfeed lists of do's and don'ts to technical instructional guides that explain the mechanics of Tweeting to websites that contain templates meant to help new users meet the formatting and rhetorical limitations of the genre.

There are several pieces of information these various articles share, including Twitter's 140-character limit (unless you use TweetDeck), how to use hashtags, how to attach photos and videos, how to re-Tweet, and common abbreviations. As Tia Fisher points out in "Top Twitter Abbreviations You Need To Know," "Twitter abbreviations and acronyms are an odd mash-up of text slang, old school chatroom phrases, common sense short forms and corporate buzzwords."

Though Tweeting may seem like second nature to you, the intricacies of Twitter communication can be quite intimidating for newcomers, particularly to people who are new to social media, in general. Just like professors have strong opinions about what it means to write academically, many Tweeters reserve strong opinions about those who Tweet without following the conventions of the Twittersphere. What becomes clear to Twitter newcomers very quickly is that the conventions of Tweets are similar to some genres they may know some about, like texting, but at the same time very different than many of the genres they were assigned to write in school. However, just like Tweeting or Facebooking, writing at the university can become quite simple, second nature even, if you're willing to take the time and make the effort to learn the conventions of the genre you're being asked to write.

. . . .

WRITE a series of three Tweets explaining to a new Twitter user how to use Twitter. Challenge yourself to do so using the conventions of the genre.

. . . .

While understanding the conventions or rules of genres is important, it is also important to know that genres change. In fact, Rhetorical Genre Studies sees genres as being in a constant state of evolution because "human activities change over time to suit new social situations and fresh challenges" (Johnson-Sheehan and Paine 2). As times and people change, so do genres. This evolution can be seen in Twitter.

As Alexis C. Madrigal points out in his 2014 article, "How Twitter Has Changed Over the Years in 12 Charts," published in *The Atlantic*:

> It's been eight years since Twitter debuted. Like the rest of the social networks that have survived, it has changed, both in response to user and commercial demands. The user interface, application ecosystem, geographical distribution, and culture not what they were in 2010, let alone 2006.

Thus, as Twitter's usage expands to new audiences and updates are made, the conventions and aims of Tweeting change. While the first Tweet, written by co-founder Jack Dorsey read simply, "just setting up my twttr," linguists, tech journalists, and Twitter enthusiasts suggest that Tweets since have become far more complex (Shontell).

Consider the various people who now Tweet and, if you are on Twitter, who you follow. Think about how different people have different purposes and audiences and how their purpose and audience shape how and what they Tweet: College students share about their day, what they're watching, reading, and listening to; Universities inform students, faculty, staff, alumni, and students' parents about what's going on at the institution and in the community; Businesses promote their services; Musicians promote their music; Celebrities share jokes, politics, and details about their upcoming projects; Politicians share their political victories, ideas, and frustrations and, selectively of course, about their lives.

So What Does All This Have to Do with Composition at A-State?

Rhetorical Genre Studies recognizes genres as socially and culturally constructed, meaning that genres are formed through compromise, negotiation, and practice of those who write and read the genre. As Anis Bawarshi and Mary Jo Reiff suggest in *Genre: An Introduction to History, Theory, Research, and Pedagogy*, "To recognize genres as socially situated and culturally embedded is to recognize that genres carry with them the beliefs, values, and ideologies of particular communities and cultures" (197). In short, genres shape your writing and, likewise, you shape genres as you write them.

Newcomers to RGS often over-simplify the pedagogy, assuming that teaching RGS is akin to teaching the traditional modes (Exposition, Description, Narration, Argumentation), but there are distinct differences. In fact, you may have had courses in which you were given the task of writing a particular essay type, like a research paper, personal essay, or a poem explication (your teacher might have even used the word "genre"), and you were likely told the requirements of the paper (length, document style, duedate, and the like), but did your teachers take the next step? Were you asked to consider questions like the following? Why and for whom does the genre exist? How do we write the genre and to whom? Who sets the conventions for the genre? How can we test the limits of the genre? Who has tested the limits of the genre? What happens when these conventions are challenged? How we can apply knowledge of this genre to other genres? Thus, RGS doesn't just teach students how to write particular genres (though that is part of it), it also emphasizes genre awareness and genre critique (Devitt 147).

As Devitt explains, "rather than being mutually exclusive, these three approaches (teaching particular genres, genre awareness, and genre critique) combine in effective college writing instruction" to:

- give students access to and control of particular genres;
- help students learn how to learn any unfamiliar genres they might encounter, whatever the medium and context;
- help students see the cultural and ideological nature of genres in order to make their own choices and gain critical understanding.

In sum, this means that in Composition I and II, writing a particular genre is important, but only a fraction of the work to be done. We fully acknowledge that we can't teach you every genre of writing you might encounter in and beyond the university. However, through exposing you to a variety of genres for a variety of purposes and audiences, such as those in this text, and engaging you in in-depth discussions about these genres, you will have the tools to discern and write the new genres that will come your way.

Works Cited

2014–2015 Undergraduate Bulletin. Arkansas State University, www. astate.edu/a/registrar/students/bulletins/index.dot.[1] Accessed 17 Feb. 2017.

Bawarshi, Anis, and Mary Jo Reiff. *Genre: An Introduction to History, Theory, Research, and Pedagogy.* Parlor Press, 2010.

Devitt, Amy J. "Genre Pedagogies." *A Guide to Composition Pedagogies.* 2nd ed., edited[2] by Gary Tate, Amy Rupiper-Taggart, Kurt Schick, and H. Brooke Heesler, Oxford University Press, 2014, pp. 146–162.

Fisher, Tia. "Top Twitter Abbreviations You Need To Know." *Social Media Today*, 22 May 2012, www.socialmediatoday.com/content/top-twitter-abbreviations-you-need-know. Accessed 2 Feb. 2017.

Madrigal, Alexis C. "How Twitter Has Changed Over the Years in 12 Charts." *The Atlantic*, 30 Mar. 2014, www.theatlantic.com/technology/archive/2014/03/how-twitter-has-changed-over-the-years-in-12-charts/359869/. Accessed 17 Feb. 2017.

Johnson-Sheehan, Richard, and Charles Paine. *Writing Today.* 3rd ed., Pearson, 2016.

Shontell, Alyson. "The First Ever Email, the First Tweet, and 10 Other Famous Internet Firsts." *Business Insider*, 23 Apr. 2013, finance.yahoo.com/news/the-first-ever-email--the-first-tweet--and-12-other-famous-internet-firsts-181209886.html. Accessed 17 February 2017.

"Twitter: It's What's Happening." *Twitter*, 2017, twitter.com/?lang=en. Accessed 17 Feb. 2017.

---

1   Notice how when you input the urls in MLA 8 you use the entire web address, with the exception of "http://."

2   Unlike MLA 7, MLA 8 asks writers to spell out roles that were previously abbreviated like those of editors and translators.

WRITE about a genre you know a lot about. You may want
to discuss Amazon reviews, text messages, or news articles.
Describe how to write successfully in this genre as though
your reader is completely unfamiliar. Your formatting and
voice should depend on the genre—a more formal genre,
like a eulogy, will likely warrant a formal voice, while a less
formal genre, like a Tweet, will likely be better explained with
an informal voice. Be sure to address the most important
conventions as well as point out the purpose and target
audience for your chosen genre. You may even want to return
to the questions raised in this section: Why and for whom does
the genre exist? How do we write the genre and to whom? Who
sets the conventions for the genre? How can we test the limits
of the genre? Who has tested the limits of the genre? What
happens when these conventions are challenged? How we can
apply knowledge of this genre to other genres?

An Introduction to Writing Narrative

Kristi Murray Costello

I still have the first narrative I ever wrote. I was in first grade and it was a story about my grandparents' cat, Zooey. It is one paragraph long and begins with the sentence, "So granma [sic] and grampa [sic] have this cat." My parents kept it all these years because the doodle of the cat at the bottom looks comically sinister and the last sentence is a blatant lie—"She is to [sic] old to fly, but she still trys [sic]." I am grateful that I have the kind of parents who knew to keep my embarrassing pictures, essays, and early novels, such as my critically acclaimed *Sunny Runs Away*, for delayed unveiling at family functions, graduations, and birthdays. Unlike them though, what I find most compelling about my narrative about Zooey the cat isn't the lie at the end or the vampire-cat drawing, but the way the essay illustrates my early understanding of the narrative genre.

At just five years old, I had already internalized an inflection and a tempo for telling a story (i.e., starting with "So grandma and grandpa have this cat..."), one that I had undoubtedly learned from listening to my parents, grandparents, teachers, and my older brother and his friends. I also used an organization similar to those I'd read in my storybooks. I began the narrative by introducing Zooey. Then, I moved into the conflict, which was that the cat wanted my cheese. Alas though, the cat couldn't get it because she could no longer fly. My point is that you already know more about narrative than you might expect and some of it you've known it for a long time.

Your experience writing narrative likely started similar to mine with short passages about your family, your best friend, what you did on your summer vacation, and what you wanted to be when you grew up. Since then, you've likely been asked to write personal essays about times you had to make difficult choices, didn't get what you wanted, or learned something about yourself. Those writing experiences have set the stage for what you'll be asked to do in this unit. That being said, while you should pull from what you learned in writing those essays as you approach your narrative essay in Composition I, you should also expect that this new assignment is going to ask you to engage with the genre in a more sophisticated way.

As you'll see from the essays and assignment prompts in this chapter, there are several subgenres of narrative, including memoirs, literacy narratives, and personal essays. As you read the essays in this section, consider each author's response to the corresponding assignment prompt and take a heuristic approach by questioning the student's work: Where and how does the essay begin? What kind of persona has the author created? How does the author develop other characters? What strategies of organization govern the essay? What kind of details does the author include? Which parts

Body Paragraph is gonna be the longest

of the story have been omitted? What techniques has the author used? How effective were these techniques? How was this student's essay a response to the prompt? Consider the differences in how you interpreted the prompt and ways that you can utilize the same techniques as you write your narrative essay. Finally, when you are given the prompt for your narrative assignment, be sure to read the prompt closely. While the differences between the sub-genres can be minimal, they can also be important.

No matter the subgenre or prompt, you can enter a narrative with the expectation that your piece should do three things:

1. Tell a story;
2. Observe details closely;   *Conventions = features*
3. Make a point.

Good narrative essays use literary elements and techniques (setting, conflict, characters, plot, imagery, dialogue) to share a true (or at least true-ish) story, but great narrative essays do all of this while also teaching us something about the writer or her unique way of seeing the world. The essays I enjoy and remember reading most reveal something bigger about humanity or identity, as in what it means to be a woman, a father, or an activist. Here's the trickiest part, more often than not, they don't even say it, but instead imply it. I think frequently about Frank O'Hara's poem, "Why I'm Not a Painter," in which he says: "My poem is finished and I haven't mentioned orange yet. It's twelve poems, I call it ORANGES." While there are times it is appropriate to have an explicit thesis in an narrative (in fact, some professors may even require it), other times it is more powerful to lead your reader to your thesis without stating it.

As you write your narrative, think about what you want the reader to gain from the essay along the way and include specific details that help lead the reader to that insight. As you decide which details to include, think about those that stick out to you most, those that feel the most authentic or poetic, and those that only you or others who were there would know. Then, share with us those sights, sounds, and smells, while simultaneously being sure not to waste your reader's time with details or pieces of information that do not deepen or further your main point. Many students ask themselves, "what really happened?" when developing their narrative, but forget to ask themselves the equally imperative follow-up question, "is it important?" Keep in mind that a critical reader will expect to find meaning in every detail.

You might be asking yourself: Will I use narrative in my daily life? When will I see this genre outside of my composition classes? Good questions. Once you're looking for it, you will see that you engage in the techniques of successful narrative on a daily basis, but, in particular, anytime you use your personal experience to substantiate a claim. Think of the

Implied thesis
hint at your Implied thesis in the introduction

Narrative

stories you tell your friends at lunch about that co-worker who annoys you or the narratives you construct about yourself on social media, in the responses you share when you are late to class, or the evidence you put forward when asking for a raise at work. Outside of your composition courses, you may be tasked with writing scholarship essays, statements of purpose, cover letters, grant applications, memos and meeting minutes, proposals, letters of support or reference, and the like. In fact, previous students of mine who have gone on to be lawyers, doctors, police officers, social workers, and teachers have written to me surprised at how often they use narrative techniques—introspection, observation, and meaning-making—in their professional lives.

If I were asked to return to my first-grade narrative about Zooey the cat, I would ask myself why I thought she could fly and what that means about my upbringing. Where did that sense of whimsy come from? I could talk about how, on those nights he didn't work, my dad read to me. He read and read until my eyes were closed and my breath was steady. We read Dr. Seuss, Shel Silverstein, *Good Night Moon*, and *Furley Cat*. Those books and that time together introduced me to worlds where anything was possible, even a flying cat. Or maybe I would write instead about how my own writing in that early essay reflects my family's storytelling traditions and how those traditions have led to my love of writing and publishing my and my family's stories. Or maybe I wouldn't focus on either of those and instead I'd talk about how my narrative about Zooey illustrates my working-class background and how, even then, at six years old, I realized the importance of working hard for what you want and the harsh reality that sometimes we want what we can't have. There are lots of threads I could follow, but a great essayist knows to choose only one.

As you approach your narrative assignment, don't pressure yourself to know exactly where you're going from the start. If you have a memory that feels significant or a question about yourself you want to explore, start writing and see where it takes you. The more I write the more I have come to realize that my best works are not the ones outlined in the first sitting, but the ones I imagine, re-imagine, and revise. Even though the planner in me tries to organize every detail of every story, the writer in me knows to take the scenic route, to hang out in my head, meander, and sometimes write 2,000 words that I will eventually cut. My high school math teacher once said, "If you pick a point, any point on a graph, there are infinite ways you can go from there." If you take anything from this introduction to narrative, I hope it's that every new occasion for writing is like a point on a graph from which you can go anywhere. It is all up to you. And, if you look hard enough, you'll see that the possibility on the page is everywhere.

Work Cited

O'Hara, Frank. *The Selected Poems Of Frank O'Hara.* Edited by Donald Merriam Allen, Knopf, 1974, New York, online library catalog. Accessed 1 Jan. 2017.

• •

WRITE about your early experiences with writing. What do you recall from these experiences? Do you remember praise or critique from those early pieces? Can you pinpoint any specific moments? Do you remember what you wrote about or whether it came easy or difficult for you? How might those early experiences have shaped your views of and approaches to writing?

• •

Narrative

Narrative

Lathan Garnett

Lathan Garnett is a 21-year-old who hails from Paragould, Arkansas, along with his parents and seven siblings. His major is Nursing and his minor is in Writing Studies. In the future, Lathan hopes to use his experience in both nursing and writing to become a writer for medical journals around the United States.

Lathan wrote this essay in Dr. Kristi Murray Costello's Advanced Composition course in spring 2016. "So often, there is such a stark contrast between the first and final drafts of students' written works, but not in this case," explained Dr. Costello. "What is published here is actually very similar to Lathan's first draft." Dr. Costello continued, "Not only was it an absolute joy to work with Lathan on this essay, but it was very clear in working with him that this was a story just waiting to be written."

The Assignment: Literacy Narrative

Write an essay about how your literacy (i.e., your reading or writing practices, perceptions or abilities, or use of or feelings about language) was shaped by your education, culture, family, or community. While it might seem intuitive to include all of these elements, instead focus on how just one aspect of your literacy was impacted by one other element. In the end, this should be a very focused narrative essay that uses your personal experience to make a broader, though perhaps implicit, argument about the nature of language, literacy, or education.

As you brainstorm for your essay, you may find it helpful to think about your literacy values and from where they originated. You may also want to consider the influences on those particular values, referred to by Deborah Brandt as sponsors of literacy, such as your parents, grandparents, siblings, teachers, and educational institutions.

Tear-Stained Pages

Lathan Garnett

Written for Kristi Costello's Advanced Composition I Course

• •

My family used to keep home videos on VHS. They have long since vanished, but I can still remember watching them as if it was yesterday. One of these video clips showed me and my father in the kitchen. In one hand, he held apple juice, in the other, milk. He would ask me in a stern voice, "Lathan, milk or juice?" Two-year-old me, thrilled that I could hear those words, would happily answer, "Milk! Juice!" Inside that video was a cute moment between father and son; outside, it was a struggle of mind over matter. It was a fight I could not win.

I was prone to ear infections as a child. At a year old my eardrums burst, leaving me deaf to the world for most of my younger childhood. My father, always believing in the power of the mind over medication, thought that my ineptitude was due to my lack of effort. I have learned not to judge my father so harshly for this; after all, he had his own share of troubles. He was once a young boy with a severe case of dyslexia. He went on to become a student who graduated from middle school, high school, and college, all without reading a book, and, as a result, he felt inadequate, as though he were not just different, but deficient.

Unlike most children, oration came to me slowly, so reading was my first real step toward conversation. It all started with what my family quaintly called the *Big Yellow Book*. My mother, as per usual, had bought the book on a whim. She was (and still is) something of a compulsive buyer, collecting things in bulk, only to leave them in the attic to rot three months later. To her, the book was nothing but a passing hobby; to me, however, it became much more than that. I would sit down with my mother and trace my finger across the *Big Yellow Book's* pages, drawing out my voice to say "mmmmm" as my finger ran under the letter "M," then sliding my finger to the "A," then the "X," sounding it out as I went along, "Max. Is. Mad." I would turn the page and a cartoonish man with steam spouting from his ears would confirm my sentence. To me, it was pure, unadulterated magic. The monotone silence that had ruled over my life vanished, and the path to language, to understanding, became just a little clearer.

Through reading, I learned that language was more than mere muffled mutterings. Language was a flowing, flowering, musical poem. Language was a knowledgeable conversation with a friend. I soon found myself conversing with Aslan about the morality of men, hands coursing through his flowing mane. I became bosom friends with Anne of Green Gables, happily

listening as a river of words fell continuously from her lips, like a bubbling brook that never ceased to flow downstream. Sometimes I would even grab a hold of some sacrilegious texts and, hidden away in my bedroom closet, follow Harry Potter into the chamber of secrets. Silence still reigned over my social interactions, but my mind was busy with heroic men and faraway lands. This made me content for a while.

Apart from the books I had read, language was still a mystery to me. At five years old, I had recovered some of my hearing, but my ability to understand others was still inchoate. My parents hired a speech therapist to develop my hearing. I remember sitting down with her one day with a box of crayons. She handed one of the crayons to me and asked, "Now, what color is this crayon?" I looked closely at the crayon before proudly exclaiming, "Vivid Tangerine!" She spent the rest of the session trying to convince me that I didn't need to read the labels of the crayons to know what color they were. It took time, but I was eventually able to carry on a conversation with her. I cannot remember her name, but I know I am indebted to her. It is thanks to her that I can speak today.

Even after all my therapy, I still carried one minute flaw: I just could not pronounce the letter "L," which wouldn't have been so bad if my name was Wathan Garnett the Third, son of Wathan Garnett Jr., son of Wathan Garnett Sr., named after a travewing vacuum sawesman. Sometimes, my father would set me in front of the bathroom mirror where he would play drill sergeant with me.

"Lathan, say 'love,'" he would say.

"Wuv." I would repeat back to him.

"No Lathan, say 'love.' No! don't look at me, look at the mirror! Watch yourself while you're speaking. Good, now say 'love.'"

"Wuv." I would reply, watching the tears well up in my own desperate eyes not daring to look away from them.

"No, Lathan, it's L-O-V-E. Say 'love'!!!"

Because of my late auditory growth, I was an awkward child. I was socially anxious and had very little knowledge of cultural norms. Suffice to say, conversation was not something I excelled in so I made it a habit to be with those who either talked way too much or way too little. I tended to spend more time around adults and infants, because they didn't demand so much from me. As a result, I made very few friends my own age. What few friends I did have didn't last long, which was fine because, since my father remodeled and sold the houses we lived in, we never stayed in one place for long. This isn't to say that I was unhappy; on the contrary, I was a very happy and optimistic child. I was of the opinion that life had too many beautiful things for me to be sad. This optimism was interrupted when I began writing.

Narrative

I first started to scrawl words onto paper at about eight years old. To this day, I am not sure why it was so difficult for me. My hands simply refused to write what my brain insisted. It certainly wasn't for lack of trying. I struggled to overcome the hurdle for six years, but to no avail. I would read books, and wonder why I couldn't do what they did. I would copy other people's writing, and watch in horror as it metamorphosed into unreadable garble by my own hand. My attempts to recreate those flowing, flowering pieces of poetry turned into grimy, soaked rhymes on paper. I would sit at the table hoping that today would be different; the result would always be a few tear-stained pages with mangled letters strewn across the paper. During those years, my mind became a clouded fog. I was sad, angry, and desperate. I had learned to understand others' thoughts, but I still couldn't portray my own through paper nor through speech.

I grew to have little self-esteem and my father grew angry at our lack of communication, demanding answers from me that I could not give. I became the child other kids avoided. I desperately wished for someone to talk to me, to understand me, but no one did, so time and time again, I returned to my books. They talked to me without requiring answers. Reading, as always, was my escape. Writing, as always, was my bane. I knew the two were linked, but could not make the connection myself. At fourteen, my mother assigned me and my siblings to something like a private school, called Veritas. Homeschooling mothers would combine their intellects to teach classes in a specialized manner. One of these teachers decided to host an English class, and my mother jumped at the opportunity. I spent the days leading up to the semester dreading the thought of going to that class and tried to convince my mother otherwise, but she was steadfast in her decision. I soon sat in a classroom full of talkative, judging teens, and we were expected to write countless papers throughout the semester.

Class started, and I waited for the first assignment, terrified. The teacher walked in, but instead of an assignment, she went to the whiteboard and started to talk about verbs, nouns, and sentence structure. I sat there, baffled, as she dissected one sentence after the next. She inserted adjectives into the sentences, lengthened and shortened sentences on a whim. It was beautiful. It was flowing, flowering poetry. It was a knowledgeable conversation. I was seeing the writer in practice, and it *made sense*. I wasn't being taught what to write, rather, I was being taught *how* to write. To the class, it was common sense; to me, it was magic.

Our teacher handed us an assignment: "Write a story," she said, and, for the first time in my life, I was ecstatic to do it. I got home and ran upstairs to my room. Shutting the door, I slid into my desk chair and threw my old, watermarked notebooks into the wastebasket. Writing was still difficult, but I had a desire to write a story like never before. And so I wrote,

Narrative

one letter at a time, "O-N-C-E U-P-O-N A T-I-M-E." Every once in awhile, I would add in one of those sentence dress-ups that she had taught us about. An adjective would give personality to that bland, dull-sounding noun. An "-ly" word would subtly add a smooth transition into those clumsy, clunky verbs. The words fell like rain, and my story, *my story*, came to life.

I spent a full day in that room writing. When I walked out, I had two pieces of weathered paper in my hands. Marks ran up and down the page. Holes were in the paper where the eraser had been time and again. It was finished and not a tear was present. I reread my work, and the result made me cringe. I had read enough books to know that it was terrible. Still, it was *mine*. My first work. Something I knew had escaped from my mind and onto a piece of paper. I had jumped the hurdle. My thoughts were free. From then on, I spent endless hours reading and writing. I took every chance I could to further my capabilities. My thoughts were free.

• •

Note: The "Big Yellow Book" mentioned in this essay refers to *Teach Your Child to Read in 100 Easy Lessons* by Siegfried Engelmann, Phyllis Haddox, and Elaine Bruner.

• •

Narrative

Narrative

BETHANY GALLIMORE

Bethany Gallimore is from Hot Springs, AR, though she's lived in many different towns around Arkansas. Bethany graduated with her Bachelors in Communication Studies and English in 2016. She wrote "A Future So Bright" in Dr. Glinda Hall's Composition I course in 2012 and is currently working on her Master's Degree in English at Arkansas State University. In her spare time she enjoys horseback riding, water skiing, travelling, and writing, and hopes to someday work in publishing or education.

Bethany is a strong proponent of the writing process, noting that her best writing is usually done through the process of long hours and many drafts. She credits Composition I and II as further aiding her development as a writer, crediting the "think-write-rewrite-edit formula" she learned from Dr. Hall as her "go-to for important writing projects."

Her advice to Composition I and II students at Arkansas State University? "Students should take notes! You may not have that one spark of inspiration again. So, jot down ideas while in class, scribble on the margins of your book, and get those ideas out and on paper."

THE ASSIGNMENT: LITERACY AUTOBIOGRAPHY

Throughout your life, many experiences, people, institutions, and texts have helped shape your trajectory as a reader and a writer. The literacy autobiography assignment asks you to consider and investigate these elements in an effort to develop a culminating argument regarding your history as a reader and/or writer. You'll note that this assignment asks you to think broadly about your experiences and their meaning, while the assignment preceding this, the literacy narrative, asks you to focus on one specific element or theme.

As you begin, explore your memory for important moments and situations that helped you develop your sense of value regarding reading and writing. As you work to focus your topic, you may also want to reflect upon the key players in your literacy that impacted your perception of writing and reading. For example, do you have fond, early memories of helping your grandmother with her Sunday crossword puzzle? Did the Pizza Hut Book Club entice you to read often and quickly? Do you recall the first non-picture book you read? What was the first book you read from cover to cover in less than a week? Or, maybe it's time look back on and reflect on how discouraged you were by your teacher's red-inked criticisms, covering the page of a story of which you'd been incredibly proud only moments before.

Narrative

A Future So Bright

Bethany Gallimore

Written for Glinda Hall's Composition I Course

• • • • • • • • • • • • • • •

My ponytails bounce against my shoulders as I run down the steps to my classroom. First day of school, first day of school! In eager anticipation I press my tongue into the gap left by my still-missing front teeth. First day of school! There is my desk, perfectly situated beneath a window that spills a welcoming light into the whole classroom. My excitement is palpable. As I take my seat my teacher hands me my first ever school assignment. "Color the school bus," she says, her eyes sparkling behind gold-rimmed glasses. So I painstakingly choose the sharpest yellow crayon out of the box, furrowing my eyebrows intently as I focus on staying precisely within the lines.

At the time, I saw nothing out of the ordinary with that first day of school. Looking back, however, I realize that my educational journey was anything but usual. The stairs I bounced down on the way to my classroom were in my own house, the brightly lit window looked out over our back yard, and the smiling, gentle teacher was my mother. I still have yet to ride on a yellow school bus like the one I so carefully colored my first day of school because I am a homeschooled student.

Contrary to popular belief, I did not go to school in my pajamas, nor did my three siblings. Every morning at 8:00, we were in the classroom with our teeth brushed, hair combed, and breakfast eaten. Mom made weekly charts with all of our assignments on them so we knew exactly what we needed to complete each day. We had textbooks, grades, essays, and extracurricular activities; we had everything except the traditional public school setting.

We were each given the option of attending public school, but none of us chose to do so. What was there to complain about when we were getting our work finished before lunch, going on the *best* field trips, and still keeping up academically with our public schooled counterparts? We would often pile in our white conversion van and set out for a day of discovery, maybe earning national park Junior

This first paragraph sets the essay in time and space. Little by little Bethany illustrates to the reader that the essay starts when she is young and embarking on her first day of school. This paragraph also establishes light as a motif.

Now Bethany steps back and reflects on her educational experiences and how they may have been different than those of her peers.

What is the impact of withholding that she was a homeschooled student until now?

In this paragraph, Bethany addresses some of the stereotypical concerns and questions people have with homeschooling. She explained in an interview, "In my experience, there is a stock of established beliefs about homeschooling that I was often confronted with as a teenager, and I wanted to dispel those ideas as soon as I introduced that I was homeschooled."

Note here that Bethany describes the "white conversion van" similar to how she describes the "yellow school bus" in the second paragraph.

Narrative

Bethany uses a long sentence here with several examples of field trips to represent the ample fun and educational opportunities she and her siblings had. Bethany further explained in an interview, "a lot of people ask me if I feel like I missed out by not having the public school experience, but honestly, I value the uniqueness of my life and wanted to show readers that not all homeschoolers live under a rock."

What similarities and differences do you see between your schooling experiences and Bethany's?

You'll see that Bethany uses several repeating sounds in this paragraph. Read this paragraph out loud. What effects do her adjectives, repeated sounds, and lists have on the reader?

Bethany chose to incorporate a joke here to let her readers know that, despite her deep love of learning, she was also a typical, silly, fun-loving kid.

Read this paragraph aloud. What impact do the repeating "s" and "c" sounds have on you as a reader?

The first sentence of this paragraph functions as a signpost to let the reader know which time frame Bethany is moving into. Bethany explained, "Since this essay covered about twelve years of my life, it was important for me to make sure my readers could follow my progression through time."

Ranger badges through studying the natural world, visiting nearby historical battlegrounds, or even taking tours of glass factories, printing presses, and television stations.

Throughout the elementary grades, Mom sat beside us at our desks, showing us how to work long division, diagram sentences, and write in cursive. But she gradually weaned us from depending on her guidance to being self-taught. By high school I was almost entirely self-motivated, finding algebra tutors, registering myself for government workshops, even preparing my own student résumé.

In my free time I was always reading, often lounging in the old wrought-iron chairs on our front porch with a furry feline purring contentedly on my lap. Books were my escape, my portal to other worlds. I read everything from science fiction to Shakespeare, realism to romance. I loved putting together family newspapers: typing up articles, inserting pictures, and experimenting with layout design. I was never very good at selling advertisements, so I wisely decided to forego entrepreneurship and allow the *Galli-Manatt Gazette* to remain a non-profit organization.

One of the advantages to being a homeschooled student was the ability to work at my own pace. I excelled in English, so I took more courses for extra credit. Math was my weak subject, so I slowed down to make sure I understood the material. I still remember staring at the clock face over my pre-algebra homework, attempting to use the evenly divided segments as an aid for fraction division. My siblings and I often encouraged one another to push beyond our supposed limits. When my younger brother did not want to stop school for the summer and began the next fall only one grade below me, I completed two grades in the same year to prove to myself that I was still his equal. My parents' plan was always for me to use that extra year to work at a job before going to college. They made a good point: I could use that time to find a job, get some real world experience, save up some money, and then go to school with students my age. But throughout high school, I found myself more and more attracted to the idea of heading directly into college.

My decision was cemented the spring of my junior year. The ACT, the final ruler to measure my academic abilities, was looming in my vision. I had always been a good student; A's were practically a requirement in our home, and I routinely scored in the top three percentile of standardized testing. But the ACT was more than just a test for me; it represented everything that I had worked for. That score was the gateway to the rest of my life. I holed up in the classroom for hours every day, poring over musty science textbooks and glossy-paged vocabulary manuals. Instead of the library's faded copy of *Hamlet*, I now perused the note-scribbled pages of *Concepts of English*. The days sped past, and soon I was driving to the high school early one Saturday morning armed with number two pencils, a plastic purple calculator, plenty of erasers, and a flock of butterflies in my stomach. As I took my seat in the testing room, I found comfort in the bright streams of sunlight determined to shine through the grease-stained windows of the old cafeteria. The light made the space seem not so unlike home.

Bethany returns to the essay's introductory image. Why and why here?

The test itself sped by in a blur of radical exponents, subject-verb agreement, and statistical interpretation. After the exam, I checked the website every day, anxiously awaiting my scores. I still remember clicking on the link one last time, dutifully entering my access code, and being faced with the most beautiful number I had ever seen. There, set in stunning white against a jet-black canvas, was my score. 30. Three. Zero. Thirty! I laughed, cried, and ended up hyperventilating in joy as I envisioned the rest of my life. With that number, I could do anything. Go anywhere, be anybody.

Bethany draws out this sentence and then breaks down the score to force the reader to slow down and read each segment of this section individually. Bethany explained, "I wanted to emphasize the importance of this score to myself and my education."

I put that number to use applying for college admittance, seeking out scholarships, and reaching out to different universities. Today that thirty, and the work it took to get there, is what allows me to attend Arkansas State University, a large step from the small basement classroom in which I was first enrolled. The crowded, echoing hallways of the student center are far different than the soft carpeted staircase outside my first classroom, and the crowded lecture halls holding hundreds provide sharp contrast with the one-on-one instruction my mother bestowed upon me. Yet every time I see rays of sunlight gently pushing their way through the classroom windows I am reminded that education is what I make of it. Whether I am in a small basement schoolroom, on the steps of a southern style front porch, or in the newly furnished desks of a university classroom, I am taking the next steps to shape, what I hope will be, a bright future.

Bethany's goal of the essay was to show how the roots of her education truly gave her advantages rather than limitations. How'd she do?

TYLER GRAHAM

Tyler has always enjoyed English, specifically writing, noting it as "the one place I can let my emotions run rampant and truly express my internal thoughts and emotions." He accredits his success and persistence in his academic endeavors, especially his writing, to his mother, who always encouraged and supported him unconditionally. He also wanted to thank his Composition teacher, Dr. Brandy Humphrey, for not only recommending that he submit this paper, but for further inspiring him to go into the field of English.

THE ASSIGNMENT: MEMOIR

Writing a memoir is more complicated than simply telling a story about yourself. Of course, as with all personal narratives, a good memoir shares a peek into the author's life; their experiences, hopes, weaknesses, fears, scars, and joys should be laid bare for the reader. A great memoir, however, doesn't simply share, it invites. The strongest memoirs take the reader by the hand and walk them through someone else's life, inviting them to participate and grow and change along with its author. A reader will relate to and enjoy a good memoir, but they will empathize and be personally affected by a great one.

For this assignment, think about a moment that affected you. This moment can be frightening or funny, intimate or public, mundane or the stuff of legends so long as it changed you or taught you something about yourself or the world around you. When you write about this experience don't just describe it, open yourself and your story up to the reader. Make yourself vulnerable and share the lesson you learned with your audience, remembering that, as a memoirist, if you do your job correctly, you're not just writing, you're teaching as well.

The Thunder Never Ends

Tyler Graham

Written for Brandy Humphrey's Composition I Course

• •

The thunder roared. My youthful wonder and my father's curiosity sent us out into the garage. We were there to watch the sky. The spring evening had been warm and relaxing as the light of day faded to twilight filtered through overcast skies, but now, the tranquility was being interrupted by Mother Nature's hostility. After she grumbled, her tears whirled in the wind and slammed against the garage. The wind-driven rain pounded the ground and whipped our cheeks. The lightning lit up our bewildered faces as we gazed into the grim and angered sky. The storm seemed like a living creature and we were aware of its power. The strength of the wind increased and the rain danced in graceful sheets in the orange hue of the streetlights. The drops danced and curled in the night before quickly vanishing as they raced from street light to darkness. The next moment seemed artificial, as if it was staged or choreographed. The lightning lit the sky as deafening thunder cracked. Wind gusted into the garage throwing us back. My dad grabbed my hand and we ran for cover.

Every time a storm came up over the mountains of northwest Arkansas, my dad and my kindergarten self were always out to watch them. Whether it be the porch or the garage, he and I would sit outside, talk, and wait for the storms to arrive. As the storm approached, our conversation would subdue and we'd switch our attention to the sky.

When my parents divorced, my mother and I relocated to Pine Bluff where her parents lived. This transitional period of time was full of chaos. Moving, meeting people, losing friends, seeing my dad less, and encountering an entirely different environment sent me into a turmoil not so unlike the storms I had grown to love. As time progressed, I continued to feel lost and didn't know my place in this new home, in a different city, surrounded by different people. But wherever I was, there was always something to see in the sky.

I read about weather, even though I was too young to understand most of the concepts, and would often look at books just for the pictures and diagrams of tornados, hurricanes, and the like in elementary school. I would try to identify cloud types and "experience" weather as much as I could, whether at recess or home. Despite all of the changes occurring, it seemed as though the weather had a certain permanency. The weather kept me focused and academically and personally engaged.

Narrative

Even as I entered middle school, I talked about weather constantly and continued to read as much as I could that I could understand. During these years, as I became more interested in meteorology and started to study it more, springtime became my favorite time of year. The storms were always at their strongest and meanest, which meant they put on the best display. As I moved into my teen years, I watched the Weather Channel when Arkansas had severe weather and would immaturely make forecasts and predictions. To my anxious mother's dismay, I stood in the garage, taking pictures and video of the storms and the lightning, despite how amateur and out-of-focus they may have been. My goal was to emulate those that I respected most: stormchasers.

On April, 27, 2011, the mid-south was forever changed by a tornado outbreak. I remember watching the devastation and horror that rose from the power of these strong thunderstorms as they ravaged several states from Arkansas to Alabama. I was horrified, but also strangely captivated. Any time tornadoes appeared on TV or people talked about them it excited me. I realized that my passion was centered on these tubes, stretching from the sky to the ground, and the storms, massive supercells, from which they were birthed. What seemed so frightening to most people fascinated me, and I wanted to witness these myself one day.

As time progressed and permanency settled on my life, I regularly saw my dad again. Back then, I didn't understand why I had to see him on weekends and then leave. It was during this time that we started to learn the basics of storm chasing. We watched many videos, from novices to well-known storm chasers and read as much as we could about the basics of meteorology and storm chasing.

During high school I advanced my education in meteorology significantly. I began to read more complicated material and started to learn the ropes of storm chasing. It was during my freshman year in high school that my dad and I planned our first chase. Armed with an iPhone and a camera, we set out to Oklahoma in March of 2012. The feeling of being out there, just my dad, myself, and the storm, among the openness of the Great Plains, was the sustenance for this growing addiction.

Our chasing endeavors really "took off" in 2013 when my dad and I embarked on several chases. When I couldn't chase with my dad, I would go with grandpa to chase the ridiculous terrain of Arkansas and the Deep South, but it wasn't the same. That was the year I realized my ultimate goal of chasing: I wanted to see a tornado. I wanted to experience the nature of the beast like the handful of chasers that regularly experienced them. I wanted to finally make what I had wanted since elementary school come true. I was by no means experienced and 2013 was my first year of truly chasing in the Great Plains. My dad and I chased several supercells that year but never got the tornado. 2014 was a hiatus in terms of chasing. We didn't go out much at all and primarily stayed in Arkansas. And my third season of storm chasing looked to be a dud as well.

Although we rebounded in 2015, chasing several times in the Great Plains and getting several incredible supercells, we just couldn't seem to get the right storm. After several failed attempts at seeing a tornado, both in and out of Arkansas, we became discouraged. I wondered if I would ever get the tornado I wanted. I even had dreams about tornadoes. When I looked at my pictures from the past I hated knowing there wasn't a shot of a tornado in that collection. It was aggravating to chase something for so long, since elementary school, and never see it. And perhaps worst of all, I began doubting my abilities as a storm chaser and forecaster.

On November 16, 2015 during my senior year of high school I finally achieved my dream. The days leading up to the 16th were screaming "chase day." All of the ingredients were there to produce tornadoes from the Texas panhandle into western Oklahoma. My dad, a friend of his, and I decided to chase that day and were determined to get a tornado on what seemed to be the last chase of the year. After chasing one storm into nightfall with no luck, we became worried that the chase would be another chase without a tornado. As we pulled off the highway to assess the situation our car became trapped in the sticky mud of a county road. With my dad at the wheel, my dad's friend and I desperately pushed and pulled on the car to get it free. Once the car was back on pavement, the situation turned ominous. The radar reported a large tornado close to where we were, but all we could see was an inky blackness.

The illumination from my laptop pierced the darkness while nervous and anxious eyes scanned the screen and sky. Piercing the nervous silence, my dad screamed "Tornado!" and my muscles contracted and eyes widened. I questioned his interjection several times testing to make sure what he saw was in fact true, but he assured me that it was. I felt absolutely sick. I missed my first tornado! Who knew how many more flashes of lightning there would be to illuminate the darkness? All eyes, camera lenses, and attention were directed towards the front windshield of the car in hopes of catching something. Then a dark mass appeared from the monotony of the inkiness of night. As lighting illuminated the looming monster from the back, we all three screamed with disbelief. We stood outside of the car, each of us with a camera in hand.

We watched the storm spin in the darkness ravaging the rural landscape through intermittent bouts of lightning. The wind screamed and pushed at our backs. The air was cool, but ribbons of warmth penetrated through. The night air was clean and crisp. We were far enough back from the storm to see its entirety, from the top of the storm all the way to the base, tornado, and the ground.

Standing in this open field I felt something I had never felt before. I felt out of myself. My body was physically there, but my mind was not. The sound around me was muted, and all other feelings I felt seemed to temporarily vanish. I felt miniscule and so obsolete compared to the beautiful force that raged in front of me. During that time there was no school, work, or worries in my personal life. All of that was gone and all that existed was the sensation of what was happening in front of me. The skies behind the storm were clear and, as a result; stars appeared as the storm moved away from us.

Since that time, I have continued to chase seasonally. The 2016 spring season was very slow to start, but in the last week of May my dad and I documented 10 tornadoes in southwest Kansas. While the rush of the chase is what I originally sought, the most important aspect to my chasing is that I'm with my dad when I do. There is no better feeling than just my dad, me, and the storms of the Great Plains. When I see a storm or chase without him it feels as if something is missing. Maybe it stems from those moments in the beginning, watching the storms in northwest Arkansas from our garage, but I'm always aware that together we can face whatever Mother Nature, or life for that matter, throws our way.

Photo courtesy of Tyler Graham

ASHLYN OREWILER

Though Ashlyn was the recipient of the 2013–2014 Freshman Writing Award, she says that writing is not a field she originally had much success in during the earlier stages of her education. She claims that this all changed with the encouragement of her Composition I instructor, Dr. Kristi Costello. It was in this Composition I course that she discovered "a certain freedom to the writing process" that allows her to express her life's experiences and love of comedy on the page.

Ashlyn draws from this experience in her advice to incoming freshmen writers. She tells them to write with creativity rather than "focusing on just getting by for a grade." She follows this up by saying, "find your own voice and write descriptively—share those details only you know."

THE ASSIGNMENT: PERSONAL NARRATIVE

Write a personal narrative that considers the relationship between a memorable aspect of your personal experience and its broader cultural, political, or humanitarian significance. The experience can be ordinary, gut-wrenching, heartwarming, heart-breaking, or even funny.

As the readings in this section will illustrate, there are a number of ways to arrange your narrative, including working from one significant event or discussing a couple of events that support one theme. As you make decisions about organization, remember that your personal narrative should do more than just tell a story, it should also make a point and observe details closely.

Pickup Parasailing

Ashlyn Orewiler

Written for Kristi Costello's Composition I Course
• •

Narrative

I see other people in the world today who are so uptight and have to do things the "right" or "safe" way. Meanwhile, sometimes I wonder if my family thinks before they do anything. Because of my upbringing, I have started to see that there are two kinds of people in this world: the thinkers and the doers. At the Orewiler household, it's clear we fall into the second category. Now don't get me wrong, I can't say that's a horrible habit to have—to do so would make me a hypocrite. After all, I am an Orewiler myself. It is true that being a doer can have many downfalls. It can result in injury, failure, or a slap from momma. Luckily though, there are many positive aspects to it as well. For instance, even if you get some broken bones or you don't quite succeed, you've still got one heck of a story to tell. And a doer loves nothing more than a good story.

Perhaps the best illustration of my family as "doer," starts with a parachute my daddy bought fifteen years ago at an army surplus store. He said he bought it to try and parasail behind his brother's ski boat. Sounds like a great idea, right? Wrong. The result was my dad being dragged face first through a massive sand castle and swallowing up enough water to run Lake Michigan dry.

My younger brother, whom I affectionately refer to as Pooky, saw this parachute one day a few years back and his eyes lit up like a cat in a room full of yarn. I could see what few gears he had in that empty head of his begin to turn. He was getting another brilliant Orewiler idea. Many people have likely had similar ideas, but then discarded them later for being too dangerous, but not Pooky. Like his father fifteen years before him, Pooky was ready to move forward.

"Dad," Pooky said, "let me strap up to this behind the truck! It will work dad! I'm so much lighter than you were. We can go out on a windy day and just try it out! Please dad! Please!"

I just shook my head and smiled. *Oh Pooky*, I thought, *that will never work. Dad wouldn't let you do it anyway since he failed at that very thing before, so why don't you put those eyes back in their sockets?*

"You know what son, I think you're right. I'll get a harness to fit you and the next windy day we have, we will test out your theory," my dad said. A smile spread across his face when he saw my surprised expression.

"Wait a minute. Do what?!" I said to my old man. "Are you serious? You tried this up at the lake fifteen years ago and, even with the outcome, you still think it can work? C'MON, Dad, think this through." I was about as shocked as I'd be if I had seen a pig fly.

Pooky didn't stop talking about it until the day arrived. You'd think it would have psyched him out, but it only seemed to fuel his excitement. In true doer fashion, Pooky's discussion of this future event never centered on the possibility that the parachute wouldn't open or other conceivable disasters, but instead on the event's potential awesomeness. In fact, the more he talked about it, I have to admit, I became a little curious myself if it would indeed work.

Finally the time came. It was a chilly day in January. The fields were sloppy muddy from a hard rain the day before. I took the truck out to one of our wheat fields and parked, while dad put Pooky in the harness. We then proceeded to get out of the truck and tie him to the hitch. If there was any fear in Pooky's heart, you wouldn't know it. The kid looked like he was about to explode with happiness. His dream of parasailing behind a pickup was about to come true.

"Alright, we're going to wait for a gust of wind, then I'll give it some gas," my dad yelled back to Pooky. "You run until the wind catches the shoot, then I'll really step on it to get you up in the air."

The wind blew open the shoot, and we were off. I was sitting in the back of the truck with a camera. There was no way I was going to miss this. Pooky took a few jogs until he flew up into the air, and I couldn't believe my eyes. He went up about twenty-five feet or so, and just when I was about to let out a victorious holler, he came crashing to the ground. He hit the dirt like a little rag doll and then was tossed back up even higher this time, only to come back down and smack the earth again. Dad kept speeding up the truck, not all that concerned his son was being thrown a mile into the ground. I can't point fingers, however, because I wasn't too concerned for his safety either. I could barely hear his thuds over my own chuckling. I could barely see him flailing through the tears of laughter running down my cheeks. I finally decided to holler at my dad to stop when I figured the poor kid had been beaten up enough. When the truck came to a halt, my brother was sitting on the ground.

"You alright, Pooky?" I yelled, trying to contain my laughter. In response, he fell over and didn't move. It might have been bad for me to get such a laugh at the expense of his wellbeing, but there was nothing I could do. When you watch someone you love do something that stupid, you just can't help it.

"Uh oh, that ain't good," I heard dad say with a little snicker as he came around the truck. What I found so funny about dad's response to Pooky's limp, lifeless expression was that he wasn't concerned he'd broke a leg or anything. He just laughed and walked out slowly to check on Pooky: classic Orewiler composure in an experiment that didn't go as planned.

It turns out the ol' boy was just fine. He was a little sore, sure, but no broken bones. We walked over to where he'd repeatedly hit the ground and there were massive ruts. When asked if he wanted to go for it again he just shook his head and widened his eyes.

Pooky's parasailing days were over.

"Just wait 'til we tell mom," I said to dad with a laugh, "she ain't gonna be too happy about this one, daddy."

In the end, there are times when I think my family is crazy, and there are times when I know it. Most people, if they considered it in the first place, would have talked themselves out of parasailing behind a pickup. Lucky for me, the Orewilers are not those people. My family is never afraid to take a chance. We will be risk takers until we are six feet under. As I look back on that day, I call it successful. Nobody died or got seriously injured, Pooky did get pretty high off the ground, and we got a great story out of it. In the end, being an Orewiler has taught me that if you think through each step of your life, weighing pros and cons, considering all the possible angles and consequences, then you can't get the rush of just flying by the seat of your pants, or in our case, by the parachute hitched to the truck. My advice? Stop overanalyzing and start doing. Who cares if it involves getting out of your comfort zone? Sometimes, you've just got to put on your big boy parachute and go for it.

Photo courtesy of Ashlyn Orewiler

Narrative

Amanda Cunningham

Amanda has won an award from the Franklin County Conservation District in Ottawa, KS as well as won first place in the State Limerick Contest in 2008. She hopes to continue her passion for writing throughout her college career.

Her paper, "Can You Hear Me?" is based on and inspired by true events Amanda has experienced. She briefly describes what it is like inside her mind living with Borderline Personality Disorder. Amanda encourages people to be open about their mental health and to not be afraid to speak up about it.

The Assignment: Behind the Moment

We've all had moments when we we've been consumed by our own thoughts. Maybe you experienced this when you proposed to your significant other, found out you'd been accepted to the college of your choice, heard your parents were getting divorced, or scored the game-winning basket in the championship game. For this assignment, you will write a personal narrative that seeks to illustrate not only the sights, sounds, tastes, and smells of one meaningful moment of your life, but also thoughts, feelings, and conflicts.

As with most personal narratives, the best memories to choose from will include some sort of tension: Will you fess up to the lie? Once you've climbed up to the highest diving board, will you jump off? Will she say yes? As you describe the memory, pay special attention to imagery and be sure to edit your draft for unnecessary repetition. You'll want to show not tell your reader your reader what happened. Help them relive your moment and see it from your perspective. Finally, try to connect your narrative to something bigger, even if your insight is implied. Maybe your narrative is meant to teach your readers about what it's like to suffer from depression, show how conflicted you were when you told your friend's secret, remind new parents that it's natural to feel distraught when your infant is crying, or explain why you skydive and engage in other rush-inducing endeavours.

Can You Hear Me?

Amanda Cunningham

Written for Leslie Reed's Composition I Course

· ·

Narrative

I open my eyes slowly. *Ugh, not again.* I look around to see where I am this time. It's dark out besides the one street lamp two houses down. I can hear the crickets chirping throughout the humid air and the buzzing of insects flying all around. There is a window directly in front of me. There aren't any lights on; it's pitch black. Suddenly there is a car light that pulls up to the front of the house and shuts off. A young girl gets out and slams the door behind her. I try to walk around to the front of the house to see the girl, but my legs won't move. I am rooted by the vehement ground. I look back into the window as I see a quick light appear. The door opens as the girl runs in, crying. She shuts the door behind her, not even bothering to turn on the light. I can hear her as she throws herself onto her bed and screams into her pillows.

I feel this sudden pain in my chest as if someone has reached in there, grabbed my heart and squeezed it. Then there is another unexpected sliver of light in the room. An older woman peeks her head through the door, "Are you okay? What's wrong?" she asks the girl in a concerned voice.

"Nothing. I don't want to talk about it."

Barely able to see what is going on through the darkness, I can instantly hear the woman's voice turn into a sharp tone, "Why don't you ever want to talk about it? I try to be here for you like you want, but you always push me away. It's like walking on eggshells around you."

"Because, Mom, when I'm upset like this I don't want to talk about it," she explains, clearly frustrated. Then with a heartfelt tone she begs, "What I want is for you to hug me, to love on me, to just sit here with me while I cry it out. Until I am ready to talk about it. I have told you this many times before."

"I give up. Plus, I can't. I have food cooking in the kitchen." The mom sighs as she turns around and walks out of the room, leaving the girl alone in the dark, deafening silence.

I can feel my heart being compressed even harder. The pain is almost unbearable. Suddenly, I hear the cries coming from the room again, or *are they in my head?* Either way, they cause my chest to get tighter and tighter. I slowly start to sink deeper into the wet, muddy pit. I begin to bang on the window for the girl to come and help me. I scream louder and louder with each breath. Still I cannot be heard over the cries. My screams, her cries, the girl are all soon lost into oblivion.

I open my eyes slowly. I look around to see that I'm in the middle of a forest. I am lost. Abruptly, I hear a voice. I'm unsure of where the voice is coming from. I whip around, *not a soul in sight. Is the voice in the sky?* I shout into the vast air, *what is going on? Who is this?*

The voice begins to speak, *Have you tried medicine? You can't just stop taking them when you feel like it. You have to keep taking it for months and months before it actually starts working.*

How do you know?! I yell back, aggravated.

Also, you should talk to someone about your...issues. A professional.

I do! Don't you understand? They all just look at me like I'm crazy! I become overwhelmed with sadness. They can't hear me—that or they never listen.

I run through the forest, hoping I will see someone. Anyone. *I want out of here!*

The voice continues. *Plus, what have you got to be sad about? There is someone worse off than you are. Think about the kids in Africa! They barely have shelter and food. You have it made. Quit feeling sorry for yourself and just be happy.*

I jump and scream. *You don't know what it's like! Do you not realize how hard I try?!* I go to strike the nearest tree, to let out my frustration. As soon as I do, something falls, hitting me on the head and knocking me out.

Ugh. I slowly start to gain consciousness again. There is a ferocious pounding in my head. I go to take a breath of air from this exhaustion that is my new life, but as I do, I am unable to breathe. A panicked feeling engulfs me. I am swimming under water. There are many people around me, but they don't seem to be struggling as I do. It's strange; I'm outside surrounded by buildings, but it is as though the world has been swallowed by the ocean. I swim up hoping there will be fresh air.

As I swim along one building, I soon hear my voice coming from one of the top windows. I swim over. *Is that me?... It's her! It's the girl.* There is no light or fight in her eyes. They are lost and sad, defeated. I realize that this girl is me. I am her. She is talking on the phone, but I can hear the other end of the conversation. *What are you thinking right now?* I ask her.

Monotone and with no effort or hope she answers, *I don't want to be here anymore. I don't want to live. There is no point. No point to me being alive.*

What are you talking about? You have so much to live for! I say, but she stares right past me, not moving a single muscle. I wish she would just listen to me. Then the lady on the other end of the phone, after a moment of silence, simply answers, "We'll meet tomorrow at 9:00 A.M. like scheduled. Will I see you then?" *Ah!* All at once and once more there was a sharp pain in my chest. I wish I had the power to just rip out my heart, *this hurts so much!*

"Sure." she replies. I know that I don't mean it. That she doesn't mean it. "I called because I was worried about you... I'll see you tomorrow then."

The water begins to fill my lungs and I am no longer able to breathe. I can feel myself slip away. Sinking back down, past the ground, everything becomes dark once again. Though feeling like this is the end of my existence, I know that I will soon be back.

Today is different. Today is nightmarish. I look around to find myself afraid of what I may find. There. I start screaming in terror, *Stop! Don't do it! Amanda, STOP!* It's useless. She can never hear me. I have no choice but to sit back and watch what is about to transpire before my eyes. Today is different. There is no pain. It's numbness, emptiness. I sit in the corner as I watch myself stir up the concoction I created over the last few days. It's like she is already gone. A tear rolls down my cheek, but I feel no remorse.

With every swallow, it gets harder and harder to watch. I go lie down, hoping the emptiness will soon vanish. Slowly, my eyes get heavier. I stare at a teddy bear across the room. My granny's bear, one of the last things my mom has from her. I think to myself, *how nice would it be to be a mother? To love someone unconditionally. If that truly is a thing: unconditional love. Rhian Elizabeth, what a beautiful name for a little girl.* With Rhian as my last thought, I drift away into oblivion once again, hoping this is it. No more sleepless nights. No more screaming into my pillows out of anger. No more walking around in a world full of happy people. No more faking smiles so it's convenient for others. No more tears. No more pain. Nothing at all.

Analysis

Analysis

An Introduction to Analysis

Elizabeth Chamberlain, Marie-Jose Patton, Tabatha Simpson-Farrow, and Mitchell Wells

Few genres are as common as analysis: Analysis is key to writing in almost every field, from engineering white papers (which analyze the implications of process or product) to business proposals (which analyze a business concept's potential for success) to literary analyses (which analyze the features of a work of fiction).

Analysis breaks down information into components, aiming to determine its essential features. So why is analysis such a significant component of your coursework? Simply put, analysis relies on the ability to think critically and process information in a manner that is both thorough and revelatory—an ability possessed by some of humanity's greatest philosophers, inventors, and entrepreneurs. The skills that you take from the analysis genre will thus be especially versatile as you continue your education into your field of study.

Analytical skills will also be useful more immediately, in other assignments in your composition classes this year, such as your argument essay or a source dialogue. Proper analysis leads the audience to the crux of a conclusion or opinion. In this sense, analysis is persuasive, and many arguments include analysis. Furthermore, one type of analysis—rhetorical analysis—actually takes argument as its focus. Rhetorical analyses examine the persuasive components of a text or image and does so by asking the following questions: How does it argue? What makes it successful or unsuccessful? How does it appeal to a particular audience? Is it credible? What sort of emotions does it make you feel? What kind of evidence does it use?

While you may not have ever done the particular kind of analysis that your composition instructor has assigned, chances are that you've been developing your analytical skills all your life. For example, before you decided to enroll at A-State you probably analyzed your options, breaking them down into factors, such as tuition, location, degrees offered, diversity, extracurricular activities and organizations, proximity to family, availability of scholarships, and so on. While you may have been accepted to another university, perhaps that institution was out of state, with raised tuition costs for non-resident students—and so, you decided to come to A-State.

Or maybe, in picking a school, you were persuaded. Maybe your best friend convinced you to come here and be her roommate or maybe the Director of Honors enticed you to enroll based on a compelling presentation on Study Abroad. Or maybe you're an online student and visited the A-State Online website, which demonstrates the university's credibility (what rhetoricians call "appealing to ethos") by telling you "you'll be part of a 100-year tradition." The site promises that you'll be making connections that will help you after college because you're joining "a robust alumni network more than 75,000 strong." But a rhetorician might be suspicious of that promise, because it's an "appeal to the bandwagon" (the rhetorical term for an argument like this: "All your friends are jumping off a cliff! You should join them!"). After studying rhetorical analysis, you will be more attentive to such appeals while analyzing a text, process, or advertisement.

Although you may have been unaware of the analytical tools you used in weighing these potentialities, you were actively engaged in analyzing information that culminated in your decision to attend A-State. Through your composition analysis assignment, you'll become more aware of your tools of analysis and learn to deploy them more purposefully.

Often, to analyze something, you'll apply a heuristic—a series of questions that walk you through breaking something down into its component pieces. For example, a heuristic for analyzing a website like the A-State Online page might look something like this:

- Who made the website? What were their goals?
- To whom is this website speaking? How do you know? How does the site specifically target that group?
- What kind of pictures does the site use? If there are people in the pictures, what do you notice about those people—age, gender, race, clothing, hairstyles, etc.?

- What kind of language does the site use? Does it speak in the first person ("I," "we"), second person ("you"), or third person (e.g., "students")?
- Consider the site's word choice. Look at particular adjectives it uses (for instance, why would the A-State website call its alumni network "robust"?).
- Consider the organization of the site. Is it easy to find the parts you need? What's first? What's last?
- Look at other features you notice—font choice, color, relative size, and so on.

Answering a list of questions like this could be the first step to writing an analysis essay. But for your essay to be successful, you'll need to do more than just answer questions. Often the biggest challenge of an analysis paper is finding your interpretive stance (that is, your main analytical point) on which you can hang all the other parts of your analysis. For the A-State Online website, you might notice that the site seems to emphasize that its online offerings are directly connected to the physical university. That could be an analytical thesis. The body of your essay would then talk about how each part of the website aims to connect to the physical university: "distinguished faculty who teach both on campus and online," the emphasis on the history of the university, and the picture of the Red Wolf Center. Another important step of analysis requires more than just dissecting a text, you've got to figure out how to connect all those parts and show how they're interrelated.

As you read the papers in this section, consider the author's response to the corresponding assignment prompt. Consider taking your own heuristic approach by questioning the student's work: How does the student present the rhetorical appeals? How do they develop their stance and in what context does their presented information interact with their source material? Consider ways that you, also, can utilize these same rhetorical tools.

By the time you leave Composition I and II, you'll have honed your analytical skills. When, in future classes or future employment, you're asked to analyze something—to write a white paper, a business proposal, a literary analysis, or any of the dozens of analytic subgenres or to analyze competing health-care plans or job candidates—think back to your practice in this class. Think about the questions you asked, the steps you took, and the ways you brought it all together.

• •

WRITE your own adaptation of the heuristic the authors of this section provide for analyzing a website for use analyzing a commercial. Then, choose a commercial that sticks out to you. Maybe it has made you laugh or cry. Maybe it irritated you or successfully convinced you to purchase a dog snuggie. Record and be ready to discuss your responses.

• •

LANDON GRIMMETT

Prior to his deployment to Iraq with the Arkansas Army National Guard, Landon Grimmett was a Disaster Preparedness Emergency Management major from North Little Rock, Arkansas. He prefers to write analytical pieces that contain subjective ideas and can be interpreted in multiple ways.

Landon advises other students to consider alternative points of view in papers and attempt to incorporate them when writing. Landon also recommends having another individual edit your papers as that person may have additional input that could improve one's work and may be able to see things you didn't catch.

THE ASSIGNMENT: LITERARY ANALYSIS

A literary analysis asks the writer to analyze a work for its literary content, focusing on the writer's interpretation of the author's work. An effective literary analysis will move beyond basic and obvious interpretation and argue for a unique way of understanding the text.

For this assignment, choose a compelling text to analyze. Read this text critically and closely. To support your thesis, refer specifically to the text, using summary, paraphrase, and direct quotation from the source as appropriate. When writing a literary analysis, it can be difficult to stay focused on the thesis. Many students are inclined to spend too much time summarizing the text. Particularly if the assigned paper is short (three pages or less) or the instructor has assigned a specific text, you will want to spend very little time summarizing and more time analyzing the text.

• •

NOTE: As you read Grimmett's essay, "The House Always Wins: An Analysis of a Fundamentalist Tradition in a Community," keep in mind that it is not your typical literary analysis as it links a literary text to traditions and beliefs enacted by a specific community within the text. Thus, it is actually more of a literary analysis/cultural analysis hybrid. In case you are unfamiliar, a cultural analysis is the study of a group's traditions, beliefs, history, interaction, folklore, and other elements that distinguish it as a community.

• •

The House Always Wins:
An Analysis of a Fundamentalist Tradition in a Community

Landon Grimmett

Written for Mark Towell's Composition I Course

· · · · · · · · · · · · · · · ·

In Shirley Jackson's "The Lottery," the villagers blindly follow an archaic tradition of human sacrifice. The end goal of the ritual is not given, but it is likely a remnant of a religious or superstitious belief previously held. Blindly following a tradition has been the cause of numerous atrocities in history. Three factors specifically affect how harmful the perception of a particular tradition can be. One factor is the repercussions of the tradition, which can manifest both as physical events and social norms. A second factor is the cultural importance of the tradition. A final and more important factor is the unwillingness of the population involved to take action if it is, in fact, harmful.

The immediate physical repercussion of the lottery in the village is the stoning of a villager every year on June 27th. In the year that "The Lottery" takes place, Tessie Hutchinson is the winner of the lottery. She is quickly stoned by the villagers and even members of her own family. Almost as brutal as the stoning itself is the normalcy with which it is carried out. The villagers assemble for the lottery and engage in small talk. There is even a moment when Mrs. Hutchinson herself causes the assembled group to laugh. She arrives late just before the drawing begins. Jackson describes the scene with Mrs. Hutchinson saying, "'Wouldn't have me leave m'dishes in the sink, now, would you, Joe?' and soft laughter ran through the crowd as the people stirred back into position after Mrs. Hutchinson's arrival" (2). The fact that they are about to kill a villager seems to have escaped the assembled villagers. The routine nature of the lottery has desensitized them to its actual effects. The villagers do not perceive it as a killing but rather as an event that is commonplace and must occur.

Analysis

A two-part title like this is common among academic papers. The first half of the title is pithy and memorable. The second half announces the purpose of the paper.

Grimmett uses here an analytic rhetorical technique called "division": He breaks up a key concept (what makes a tradition harmful) into several parts. Note the way that division lets him interrogate the idea that a tradition might be harmful from different angles. Consider how this introductory paragraph connects his interpretation of "The Lottery" to his broader analytic point about harmful traditions.

This phrase creates a hierarchy among Grimmett's three major points.

Note how this sentence serves to preview the details to come. The summary and quote that follow both demonstrate the "normalcy" of the stoning.

This signal phrase identifies both the author of the story (Jackson) and the character speaking (Mrs. Hutchinson).

Grimmett offers a lot of detail to demonstrate the "normalcy" with which the brutal stoning takes place. Yet he does not return to the original question of this paragraph: How immediate physical repercussions (such as stoning) affect the potential harm of a tradition. How could he make a clearer connection to the overall purpose of the paragraph?

The cultural importance of the tradition also impacts the perceived morality of it. Even though the lottery is commonplace, the villagers clearly have a reverent, procedural attitude towards it. Jackson writes, "There was a great deal of fussing to be done before Mr. Summers declared the lottery open" (2). Later in the paragraph, Jackson lists different tasks that must be completed in preparation for the lottery. Another instance of the villagers' reverence toward the lottery occurs after the black box is introduced. Jackson writes, "Mr. Summers spoke frequently to the villagers about making a new box, but no one liked to upset even as much tradition as was represented by the black box" (1). While the villagers still maintain a reverence toward the lottery, they have lost a good deal of the actual ceremony associated with it. Jackson writes, "At one time, some people remembered, there had been a recital of some sort...but years and years ago this part of the ritual had been allowed to lapse" (2). This line shows the passive attitude the villagers have in regards to upholding the tradition of the lottery. While they still believe that the lottery is important, they have effectively lost the root of the tradition. This is also evident in the fact that the purpose of the lottery is never stated.

Is Grimmett is suggesting that, if the tradition was better-rooted in ceremony and history, it might have been more acceptable?

A final and more important factor is the unwillingness of the population involved to take action. Jackson illustrates this point with dialogue between two characters, "'Some places have already quit lotteries,' Mrs. Adams said. 'Nothing but trouble in that,' Old Man Warner said stoutly. 'Pack of young fools'" (4). Even with the knowledge that other villages have quit lotteries, the villagers continue theirs. Old Man Warner even goes so far as to label other villages as a "pack of young fools" (4). This is indicative of a fundamentalist attitude and has been prevalent in history. Old Man Warner dismisses any alternate position as a younger generation disrupting the existing status quo. While the lottery could potentially affect any of the villagers, they distance themselves because each year they have remained unaffected. A quote from Martin Niemoeller regarding the persecution that occurred in the Second World War illustrates this point:

How is Grimmett using this term? What does it mean for his purposes?

First they came for the Communists, but I was not a Communist so I did not speak out. Then they came for the Socialists and the Trade Unionists, but I was neither, so I did not speak out. Then they came for the Jews, but I was not a Jew so I did not speak out. And when they came for me, there was no one left to speak out for me. (Niemoeller)

This position is evident when Mrs. Hutchinson is stoned by the villagers and she asserts, "It isn't fair, it isn't right" (Jackson 7). Even as the other villagers must surely be able to empathize with her position, none are willing to challenge the established tradition. This creates a vicious cycle where the youth are indoctrinated with the social norms established, thus ensuring the norms continue.

Notice how Grimmett turns back to the story he's analyzing here, making a connection between the Niemoeller quote and Jackson's narrative.

The villagers in "The Lottery" execute their tradition as is customary. They do so without a stated purpose and to deadly effect. The tradition results in the murder of one villager every year and the desensitization of the survivors to the ritual. While the villagers appear to maintain some reverence toward the tradition they have lost many ceremonial elements as well as the root purpose. The villagers are also unwilling to challenge the established status quo in regards to the tradition and instead allow the heinous acts to be committed. These factors and the actions of the villagers ensure that a harmful tradition will continue to exist.

Remember Grimmett's stated purpose: To demonstrate the three key factors that affect how harmful a tradition may be, through analysis of "The Lottery." Connecting cultural analysis to literary analysis is a challenge. How successful is he at making that connection? Is this a better literary analysis, or a better cultural analysis?

Analysis

Works Cited

Jackson, Shirley. "The Lottery." English 1003, *Blackboard*, 13 Feb 2015.

Niemoeller, Martin. "Martin Niemoeller: (1892–1984)." *Jewish Virtual Library: A Project of AICE*, American-Israeli Cooperative Enterprise, Jewishvirtuallibrary. org.

· ·

Note: When inputting URLs in MLA 8 you use the entire web address, with the exception of "http://."

· ·

CAROLINE PULLIAM

Caroline has always identified herself first as a dancer, then as a student. For the entirety of her high school experience, dance filled all of her time. She cannot imagine going more than a day or so without dancing or practicing her dancing 20–30 hours a week. The stress of daily living combined with the anxieties of simply growing up were always quieted by the structure and consistency of dancing. However, during her senior year, she realized how much she enjoys writing as well.

It has always seemed easier for her to write essays than for her classmates, but she hasn't always necessarily enjoyed the practice as she does now. She sees writing as creative and relaxing rather than something she'd like to pursue as a professional pursuit, though she hopes to see her "appetite for this calming method of creation grow."

THE ASSIGNMENT: RHETORICAL ANALYSIS

Your narrative assignment helped you to find your voice as a writer and learn to support a claim with your personal experience. This assignment requires you to use that voice to make a claim about a text. You will choose one short text to dissect. To begin, ask yourself questions like: What is this text trying to do? With whom is it trying to connect? How effective are these efforts? It sounds simple, but it can actually be quite difficult because we are more accustomed to analyzing meaning, as opposed to intention and effect. In fact, students often believe the rhetorical analysis to be the most difficult assignment in Composition I.

To ensure that you can really dig deeply into the text, you'll want to choose a written text that is three pages or fewer or a video that three minutes or fewer. Be sure the text is something that excites you or has an interesting element upon which you would like to focus. Finally, keep in mind that not all members of your audience may have seen your chosen piece, so at the beginning of your analysis, you should explain it briefly to the audience. Do be careful that your summary of the piece does not take up valuable room in your paper which should be reserved for analysis.

After annotating your text and mapping out the author's uses of rhetorical devices (ethos, pathos, logos, kairos), look for connecting themes or a unique angle you can focus on to unify your thesis. Your thesis should express your main point and prove something to the reader about the meaning behind the text that they may have not seen otherwise. Thus, this assignment may require you to do some research, but do remember that your argument must pertain to the text.

The Law of Human Nature

Caroline Pulliam

Written for Tabatha Simpson-Farrow's Concurrent Composition I Course

Morality is a subject always up for debate. While various works serve to spark this ambiguity in their readers, the texts of C.S. Lewis aim to answer the questions generally posed by other philosophers, writers, and altogether intellectuals. This matter so often argued (and always with passion in one direction or another) is clarified using logos significantly more than any other appeal in "The Law of Human Nature," the first chapter of Lewis's *Mere Christianity*. His use of diction, along with the success of his other works, also contributes considerably to his credibility by creating a specific tone.

Lewis defines the Law of Human Nature as a ruling without which people could "fight like animals, but they could not quarrel in the human sense of the word" (11). Rather than appealing exclusively to, or at least directly toward, a fellow Christian or religion critic, he writes for the *reader, any reader's* understanding of the point which he is making. His audience is directly addressed, and he leaves no room for interpretation in his syntax.

This tone is exemplified through the manner in which he presents the purpose of the chapter. He categorizes it into two points: "First, that human beings all over the Earth have this curious idea that they ought to behave in a certain way and cannot really get rid of it. Secondly, that they do not in fact behave that way. They know the Law of Nature; they break it" (13). Lewis proceeds to prove this through what by and large becomes a reasoned basis for faith in any theism (not Christianity alone), thus fulfilling his objective for this particular work as a presentation of justified ideas with the intention of promoting and defending God, or what is commonly known as a Christian apologetic.

"The Law of Human Nature," however, does not in itself meet the definition of a Christian apologetic. It only sets the stage for the rest of the book by using reason, which plays an immense role in Lewis's entire argument. He presents undeniable truths to form a strong logos and supports this with examples which appeal to all humans. In one example, Lewis asks, "What is the sense in saying the enemy were wrong unless Right is a real thing which the Nazis at bottom knew as well as ought to have practised [sic]?" (12). He mentions the German genocide because it serves as a legitimate representation of this theory in that so many people collectively and resolutely disagreed with what the Nazis were doing, that the outcome was world war.

Analysis

There will be those who feel that Lewis's beliefs regarding the supernatural greatly affect his opinion in this argument, a perspective based on his past novels and memoirs. They will then pose the question: *Is this chapter, this entire book, truly an unbiased evaluation of the manners in which humans function on the basis of morality, or is it merely a reflection or spillover of his being at a loss to writing anything other than the Christian works which have been so successful for him in the past?* However, after looking into Lewis's life, not only a writer, but also as a person, it becomes evident that he truly understood the controversy from both sides. After all, he was an atheist for many years before he committed himself to faith.

Lewis displays an understanding of his opposition's beliefs while explaining without bias why those opposing views are deniable and rendered invalid in his statement, "I know that some people say the idea of a Law of Nature or decent behavior known to men is unsound, because different civilizations and different ages have had quite different moralities" (12). He combats this idea by challenging the reader to identify what an entirely different morale would resemble. Then he uses logical examples that unify various religions, culturally distinct nations, and time periods under one general conduct of virtue when he writes, "Think of a country where people were admired for running away in battle. Selfishness has never been admired." (12). These behaviors are frowned upon in any society because they are a submission to the weak-minded instincts of the body, whereas people who are brave or selfless are consistently credited for the strength of their mind.

Lewis points out that these weaker instincts, when acted upon, are viewed as undesirable and symbolize the flaws in human nature which are identified by all civilizations. He uses pathos in his claim, "Excuses are proof of how deeply, whether we like it or not, we believe in the Law of Nature...we cannot bear to face the fact that we are breaking it" (13). He also appeals to every person, for every person has made an excuse for some poor act or another, regardless of where it stands (on whatever preferred scale) immorally, and every person therefore finds this example relatable, which contributes to the effectiveness of his claim.

Photo courtesy of Caroline Pulliam

Furthermore, his assertion does not stand alone in terms of relativity. Lewis does not excuse himself from these claims, stating, "I am just the same" (13). Because of this, much of his credibility lies in his ability to remain unbiased in his argument. By including himself in the generalized group of humans, he collectively clarifies his objectivity and establishes his ethos. By using pronouns such as "we" instead of "you" or "people," Lewis strengthens his credibility with readers, saying, "we have failed to practice ourselves the kind of behaviors we expect from other people" (13). In this way, readers know that he has failed just as many times as they have.

In his opening chapter, C.S. Lewis laid the foundation upon which the rest of his book stands by successfully and arguing the Law of Human Nature from a refreshingly logical, unbiased standpoint. By using logos, ethos, and pathos in his assertions and maintaining an objective tone through clear and direct diction, he proves that humanity can be united under one generalized sense of morality, thus effectively opening the minds of his readers as he leads them into his real argument: the consideration of Christianity.

Works Referenced

"Christian Apologetics Questions and Answers." *Creation.com*. Creation Ministries International, 2016, creation.com/christian-apologetics -questions-and-answers.

Lewis, C. S. "The Law of Human Nature." *Mere Christianity*. Edited by Geoffrey Bles, HarperCollins Publishers, 1952, pp. 1–20.

• •

NOTE: The reference page that accompanies this work is a Works Referenced page instead of a Works Cited because the term "Works Cited" refers specifically to a list of sources cited in the text. For instance, any work which is directly quoted in a text would be marked by a parenthetical citation. This citation can then be linked to a specific entry in a Works Cited page. A Works Referenced page is a place to list works which were consulted, but not directly quoted or specifically discussed within our work. Writers should be careful to recognize the distinction between the two types of reference pages and list sources accordingly.

• •

MOHAMMED GHIAS

Mohammed is currently a junior majoring in Accounting at Arkansas State University. He is well-traveled and possesses a diversity of skills. He was born in Kuwait, lived in Canada, and is originally from Pakistan. He has a passion for travel and exciting adventures.

Mohammed loves knowledge and believes it is the most powerful tool a person can possess. In order to learn anything and be successful in it, Mohammed believes that one must not only have a passion for knowledge one might gain, but also for the love and kindness that the person will spread by helping others through employing that knowledge. For this reason, Mohammed will continue his education and pursue a doctorate in the future.

Mohammed had this to say about writing: "Writing is a very efficient way to express oneself. By thinking slowly and carefully, one is able to vent out all of his or her emotional exhaustion and can plan and decide·on important life decisions. Not only does writing make one a better communicator, but it also can put him or her in a better mood. How is it possible to achieve this in academic papers? If there is something that a person can relate to or that evokes certain feelings, he or she will become more interested. Connecting with people through writing is the most important step to getting one's points across and making them understandable and interesting. They should be introduced at the beginning of the paper to get the person 'hooked.'"

THE ASSIGNMENT: RHETORICAL ANALYSIS

Rhetoric is the art of using language and media to achieve particular goals. Thus, a rhetorical analysis is an argumentative essay that takes a close look at the strategies of persuasion within a text and makes an argument about the use or effectiveness of said strategies. When you write your Rhetorical Analysis assignment, you must take words seriously, know your audience, and read closely so that you can offer strong claims about the text and support those claims with textual evidence. Thus, you aren't simply deciphering the meaning of the text, rather you are taking the text apart to see how it works (or doesn't). When writing a rhetorical analysis of a text, the writer needs to ask herself who the author is writing to, how she attempts to appeal to the reader's feelings (pathos), intellect (logos), sense of self (ethos), and how effective these attempts are.

For this assignment, you will choose a short text (no more than three pages long, if written, and no more than four minutes long for videos or podcasts) to dissect, analyze, and write about. Ultimately, you will want to make an argument that is greater than the sum of its parts (i.e., your thesis should be more nuanced than "This article utilizes ethos, pathos, and logos.").

Samsung Galaxy S6 Plays It Smart

Mohammed Ghias

Written for Kerri Bennett's Summer Composition I Course

• •

Today smartphones are indispensable, and, therefore, smartphones are in high demand. Smartphone companies battle each other to sell more products than their competitors, and since all smartphones' functionalities are the same, companies rely on gimmicky commercials to aggrandize ordinary features in order to persuade as many people as possible to buy their products. The commercial for the new Samsung Galaxy S6 is a perfect example of a smartphone company trying to persuade people to buy a product that performs identically to other, older smartphones. However, the commercial cleverly combines ethos, logos, and pathos to successfully persuade its audience to buy the product.

The company, Samsung, is enormous and produces not only smartphones, but also a variety of home appliances, so the name is well-known around the world. Because of its vast electronic offerings, the company has many loyal customers. Samsung's Galaxy line is its top-of-the-line, flagship smartphones, and the phones are targeted toward all groups of people. The company releases a new Galaxy S series every year, and this year, it debuted the sixth iteration: the Galaxy S6.

The commercial begins by using ethos, displaying the text, "Introducing the All-new Samsung Galaxy" (Easy2plaYFullHD 0:01). Because of the credibility of the Samsung Galaxy name, audiences immediately recognize that the commercial is from a renowned company which is introducing its flagship smartphone. The company has chosen to use fancy color names to make its product sound luxurious: "Black Sapphire, White Pearl, Blue Topaz, Gold Platinum, and Green Emerald" (Easy2plaYFullHD 0:37). Samsung is saying that consumers can experience these luxurious items without actually having to spend a small fortune. Toward the end of the commercial, detailed specifications of the device are shown, which only tech-savvy people can understand, thus appealing to this segment of the audience. In considering Samsung's ethical standing, we can deduce that the commercial is geared toward a variety of people: different socioeconomic classes, general users, and advanced users.

To attract the majority of the audience, which is general or regular users, the commercial attempts to appeal to viewers' logical reasoning. Early on, the commercial indicates that the device is "crafted from metal and glass" (Health and Fitness 0:10). From this, the audience is able to construe that the device is durable, luxurious, and modern. The commercial

then shows scenes of typical smartphone features in real life usage, illustrating that the device is simple to use in everyday settings, produces professional results, and is aesthetically pleasing. Each scene describes the device's detailed specifications, along with its overall advantages, using simple language so that the general users can understand.

The commercial also uses the concepts of dissonance and consonance to introduce this flagship device. In the beginning, the commercial uses dissonance by combining a dark background color and heavy, deep sounds to induce tension and curiosity. This gives viewers the feeling that something very sophisticated is about to be introduced and that it is something out of this world. The tension generated through that sense of dissonance is then resolved in the second part of the commercial, which gradually shifts to a more pleasant tone, showing fully colored scenes of people using the device productively. This gives the feeling that an ethereally designed device has landed in the person's hands. This additional appeal to the viewers' emotions is used here as an add-on to make the unveiling of Samsung's flagship device feel more dramatic and to accentuate the logos and ethos used in the commercial. This tactic also serves to attract all types of people.

Typically, all smartphones have similar features, such as web-browsing, access to apps and music, as well as various utilities. It is the way a company presents its products that differentiates those products from others and provides a competitive advantage. Commercials try to aggrandize the typical smartphone features by using strategies to make them seem revolutionary. By effectively and strategically combining ethos, logos, and pathos, the Samsung Galaxy S6 commercial successfully persuades different groups of people to purchase the product.

Works Cited

"Samsung Galaxy S6 and S6 Edge Commercial 3." *YouTube*, uploaded by Easy2plaYFullHD, 2 Mar 2015, www.youtube.com/watch?v=uLE82S3a06c.

• •

NOTE: For help developing a thesis for a rhetorical analysis, see the writing prompt that follows Carmen Williams' process analysis, "How to Explain *50 Shades of Gray* to an Octogenarian."

• •

MAZIE TACKETT

Mazie Tackett is a student at Arkansas State University majoring in psychology. Alongside her psychology degree, she has also chosen to minor in creative writing, which she hopes to use in conjunction with her field of interest. She explains, "I want to go into therapy to help people. I want to use writing as a door to help people find a safe place to discover their own voice and let out their true thoughts."

THE ASSIGNMENT: RHETORICAL ANALYSIS

A rhetorical analysis looks deep into a text in order to make claims about the strategies of persuasion used within the text and their effectiveness. Thus, you aren't simply deciphering the meaning of the text, rather you are taking the text apart to see how it works (or doesn't). When writing a rhetorical analysis of a text, the writer needs to ask herself who the author is writing to, how she attempts to appeal to the reader's feelings (pathos), intellect (logos), sense of self (ethos), and how effective these attempts are.

For this assignment, you will choose a short text (no more than three pages long, if written, and no more than four minutes long for videos or podcasts) to dissect, analyze, and write about. Ultimately, you will want to make an argument that is greater than the sum of its parts (i.e., your thesis should be more nuanced than "This article utilizes ethos, pathos, and logos.").

Note that your instructor may apply a theme or other parameters to your selection. For example, Mazie and her classmates were instructed to choose a text pertaining to the 2016 election, such as an op-ed, campaign ad or commercial, political apology, Tweet, speech, or debate. As you can see, there are a number of mediums available for this assignment, so the author was able to get creative.

UNITED States of America

Mazie Tackett

Written for Robin Everett's Composition I Course

· ·

The *YouTube* video "What Abe Lincoln Prophesied about Trump and Hillary" is hosted by an incredibly popular and well-known (and equally long-dead) president, Abraham Lincoln. It opens with a familiar man in a black coat and top hat whom various generations could easily identify as Abe Lincoln. However, the dialogue attributed to this "pillar of respect" is not what one would expect. The Balanced Rebellion, a *YouTube* channel created to promote a particular presidential candidate, brings in a legend known through the ages to unify the audience, then modernizes him to grab and keep the audience's attention. The video begins by criticizing and ridiculing the two main candidates in the 2016 U.S. presidential race, Hillary Clinton and Donald Trump. The video attempts to reduce the candidates' credibility before even mentioning Gary Johnson, who is presented as an alternative presidential candidate. Humor is used throughout the ad to lighten the mood and keep the audience attentive. The Balanced Rebellion doesn't try to pull on the audience's heart strings, nor does it drone on with information the audience might not understand. The Balanced Rebellion uses Abraham Lincoln effectively to grab the audience's attention. This is a good strategy because it uses something well-known and something that will bring the audience together instead of apart. It also relies on humor instead of anger, fear, or sadness to keep the audience laughing and focused on the content of the message.

The ad begins, "Oh, hey America! It's me, dead Abe Lincoln..." (Balanced Rebellion 0:02). While having Abraham Lincoln speak for Gary Johnson helps build up credibility for Johnson, the audience is aware that Lincoln isn't actually supporting Johnson because Lincoln is dead. Johnson needs credibility because he is not a Democrat or a Republican. He is a Libertarian, which is a third party, or minority political party in the U.S. Though a third party presidential candidate has not won before, currently, the nation is divided between supporters of "a corrupt president or a crazy president" (Balanced Rebellion 0:08). Making him a third option instead of those unpleasant choices gives Johnson a bigger chance of actually being considered for the presidency. However, this isn't the first time the nation has been divided over politics. Seven score and sixteen years ago, the conflict over slavery split the nation in two, but Lincoln was able to mend the division, uniting the nation once again. Because of this, Abraham Lincoln is a figure that is taught throughout school, a figure most Americans know,

and he represents an idea that most people understand, relate to, and like. The Balanced Rebellion hopes viewers will think of these same attributes when they think of Johnson, and maybe then they will choose to vote for him.

Audiences can relate to honest, dark, and nonsensical humor, and this is another way The Balanced Rebellion grabs the audience's attention and keeps it. These kinds of humor tend to get one to think further about a joke, as opposed to a normal wisecrack. As Abraham Lincoln ridicules both Trump and Hillary, he uses honest, dark, and occasionally nonsensical humor. He uses the honest humor most often with Hillary. He says, "First there's Hillary, who's like a monopoly player, using her get out of jail free card, then her rig an election card and make millions on political favors card" (Balanced Rebellion 0:20). This, itself, is ironic because he uses honest humor to get the audience to think deeper into Clinton's position, while also laughing. While the main purpose of the comment is to make the audience laugh, there is an element of truth underlying the joke. In contrast, Lincoln uses nonsensical humor with Trump. Lincoln does this by calling him the "crazy president." By using humor that doesn't really seem to fit into the situation such as the phrase "one horse eats Muslims," Lincoln attempts to make Trump out to be an outrageous clown. Furthering this humiliation, Lincoln states, "Then there is Trump, who's like if your racist uncle got drunk and ran for president, and then the nation got drunk and said, 'that guy should have nuclear bombs'" (Balanced Rebellion 0:27). In this quote, Lincoln claims that Trump is a racist. While he does use humor, Lincoln points out the underlying horror of a drunk racist having access to nuclear bombs. Lincoln then uses sarcasm to imply that the nation would have to be drunk for Trump to become president.

According to Lincoln, Trump isn't a fit choice, but neither is Hillary. In the next part of the video, he contributes to both ethos and pathos. He grabs the audience's attention and holds it by comparing Trump and Hillary to famous comic villains and portraying America as the beloved Gotham City from the DC Comics universe. "If America is Gotham city, then Hillary is the mob and Trump is the Joker" (Balanced Rebellion 1:00). Through these representations, Lincoln shows how Hillary and Trump are tearing the nation apart in the same way that the corrupt mobsters and the Joker attempt to destroy Gotham City, and neither one should be voted for. Lincoln adds to his own credibility by connecting with his audience's interests as a whole, and once again bringing them together under a common knowledge. While making himself more relatable, Lincoln also unravels both Trump's and Hillary's credibility by comparing them to well-known villains. This comparison makes the audience question where the hero is.

Analysis

Lincoln does not hesitate to answer: "It's time to vote for freaking Batman!" (Balanced Rebellion 1:16). Immediately after that, Gary Johnson is mentioned in the video for the first time, connecting him, in the audience's mind, to Batman. As Hillary is the mob, and Trump is the Joker, this logically leaves Gary Johnson to save the day as Batman. Lincoln then explains how a third-party candidate can actually win now, and instead of skipping the issues, Lincoln pays close attention to details, starting with the economy. He starts with the other candidates, explaining how Hillary wastes money on a "NASCAR jacket to show off her sponsors" (Balanced Rebellion 2:56). Then Lincoln exposes all of Trump's business failures, comically listing them off one-by-one, and tying it altogether with, "Trump: the board game, which is apparently a game where you suck at business naming things after yourself then become president" (Balanced Rebellion 3:08). This, once again, makes the audience laugh after a long list of details. After illustrating the other two candidates' faults, Lincoln uses the opportunity to highlight Gary Johnson's success as governor of New Mexico and says that unlike Hillary, "the mob," Gary Johnson doesn't waste money on useless things. The video states, "He cut taxes 14 times and still left the state with a $1 billion surplus," and unlike the Joker, Trump, Johnson wasn't destroying everything he touched (Balanced Rebellion 3:17). He built "new highways, bridges, schools, and hospitals" (Balanced Rebellion 3:22). They should give him a cape and call him Batman!

But heroes don't always wear capes, do they? The next issue Lincoln covers is national defense. He says, "Trump and Hillary are both pro-war" (Balanced Rebellion 3:30). Lincoln then lists several things that Hillary and Trump have supported, which have cost several heroes' lives. Next, Lincoln looks to the audience and says, "So you can choose the lady who helped create ISIS or the guy that talks like he's in ISIS" (Balanced Rebellion 3:47). At this moment, Lincoln uses several different emotions to get a reaction out of the audience. While Lincoln uses dark humor to make the audience laugh, he is clearly also angry at these two candidates—angry that Trump and Hillary are thought to be the only two choices. Furthermore, Lincoln mentions that Johnson is the most popular candidate with the troops. This makes it evident that Johnson wants to end wars. He wants to make things safe, and war doesn't equal safety. Johnson tells an interviewer in *The New Yorker* that he detests war and the taking of innocent lives. He claims, "The unintended consequence of when you put boots on the ground, when you drop bombs, when you fly drones and kill thousands of innocent people— this is resulting in a world less safe, not more safe" (Lizza 1).

To make things better at home, the nation needs to be united once again. The Balanced Rebellion not only incorporates this idea into its words,

but also into the video as a whole. The video uses ideas and references that everyone can understand, so no one is left out. Each insult and ridicule Lincoln uses is deliberately selected to depict two sides, two hands, each holding one side of a piece of paper ripped down the middle. Both hands are clutching their piece tightly with sharp claws. These hands carelessly ripped a delicate, beautiful thing in two, and instead of trying to make it whole once again, they hoard over the little piece they have. This image symbolizes Johnson's views of Trump and Hillary. Instead of grabbing for a piece of the already torn America, Gary Johnson wants to be the glue that puts it back together. Repeatedly, this video illustrates the same sad picture. It shows two greedy hands, pulling the nation farther apart. Then the glue comes in, trying to find ways to close the gap the others have created. During this video, Abraham Lincoln repeatedly refers to this country as "just America" rather than "The United States of America" because right now, this country is "just America" and not united at all. However, this ad is effective because for a few short minutes, Lincoln makes the viewer aware that we aren't "just America," but that we need to once again be the United States of America.

Works Cited

Lizza, Ryan. "The Libertarians' Secret Weapon." *The New Yorker*. 18 July 2016.

"What Abe Lincoln Prophesied About Trump and Hillary." *YouTube*, uploaded by Balanced Rebellion, 25 Aug. 2016, youtu.be/GLAh3pui-CI.

Photo courtesy of Mazie Tackett

CARMEN LANOS WILLIAMS

Carmen Williams is an instructor of composition and literature at Arkansas State University as well as a Ph.D. student in A-State's Heritage Studies Program. She studies African American literature and heritage sites in the Delta region.

Carmen wrote this essay not only to expose her students to the process analysis genre, but also so that she and her students could engage in rhetorical analysis of the essay together. Since the rhetorical analysis is an assignment with which many students struggle, Carmen aimed to make the essay engaging and funny.

THE ASSIGNMENT: PROCESS ANALYSIS

A process is a series of actions that usually leads to the same result, no matter how many times they are repeated. A process analysis explains such a process by breaking it down into a fixed order of detailed steps.

For this assignment, you will write a process analysis that either supplies detailed directions for replication of a process or information about how a process works or is done. Like narration, the process analysis will need clear, pertinent details, examples in each step, and transitions that help your reader move from one step to the next. Your paper should also include a thesis statement or an implicit main idea that explains what your audience will gain or learn by following your process. Some questions you may want to consider as you choose your topic are as follows: What processes do I take part in daily? What skills or knowledge do I possess that are unique and have interest to me and others? What ceremonies, traditions, or rites of passage have I experienced? What is an impressive process I have witnessed or experienced? What is an ineffective process I have witnessed or experienced? What steps could be taken to make this process healthier, safer, more efficient, or more manageable? And, what kinds of process analyses, or "How To" pieces, do I enjoy and why?

Consider what you know about your audience as you write. Arkansas State University students (and faculty) are bright and intellectually curious—they know a lot about many things—but they don't know everything about everything, which means that, even if you are writing for the A-State First-Year Community, you may need to explain key concepts and define terms.

How to Explain *Fifty Shades of Gray* to an Octogenarian

Carmen Lanos Williams

Written for her Composition I and II Courses

· ·

Analysis

A few weeks ago, my grandmother was watching *Good Morning America* and learned that actors had been cast for a film version of the best-selling book, *Fifty Shades of Gray*. She asked me, "What is *Forty Shades of Gray*?" My jaw dropped and I chuckled nervously, struggling to find the right words to explain this notoriously raunchy text. I mean, can you really have a detailed discussion about erotica with a person in her eighties without traumatizing each other? The answer is, yes, if you are creative enough.

Before getting into the gritty details of the story, quickly reflect on the relationship that you already have with the octogenarian: Is she your BFF, your grandma, the old lady at the gym who consistently tries to set you up with her grandson? These things matter. If she's a friend, it might be far easier to discuss this with her. If she's your grandma, you are opening yourself up to judgment, or even worse, sex stories about her and your grandpa.

Explore this relationship further. Have you ever discussed "dirty stuff" with her before? If you haven't, then you will need to modify the potentially offensive parts. Here's a simple test. If she has routinely watched *Sex in the City*, *Girlfriends*, *Girls*, or even *The Golden Girls*, you may proceed with the details (adulterated or unadulterated). If she doesn't watch shows like these or, worse, if she's disgusted by shows like these, then you're going to have to change up the plot, just a little bit, to accommodate a person who identifies more with a Puritan than with Carrie Bradshaw.

After evaluating the degree to which you can discuss sex with the octogenarian, the next most important part of explaining *Fifty Shades* is to focus on the elements of the story that have little to do with sex. In short, be selective about the details you emphasize. Forget about the pesky SMBD lingo and explain the plot by highlighting the virginal heroine's struggle to love a man who wishes to dominate and control her. Then, to justify why you would root for such a mismatched, misogynistic relationship, you will need to frame Christian Gray, not as a submissive-turned-dominant, but rather as a man with a troubled past whose desires to control Anna are rooted in trying to protect her and to avoid losing her love.

If you find that talking about the plot makes you too uncomfortable, go directly to the happily-ever-after ending. Be sure to emphasize that Anna reforms Christian, the two get married, and start a family. You might also emphasize that yes, Anna loses her virginity to Christian, but she also ends up marrying him.

Now, here's where it gets complicated. If the octogenarian suspiciously asks you why it took three books to tell such a "simple" story, you can do one of two things: 1) say something like, "people these days drag everything on, don't they?" and hope that it turns into a conversation about the current awful state of the world (which many old people LOVE to discuss) or 2) you can tell the truth. I suggest the first because if you choose the latter, you have to be prepared to define concepts like "dominant," "submissive," and "safe-word."

Finally, I must caution you not to sugarcoat *Fifty Shades* too much. Things could backfire and she might insist on reading it. This could lead to greater embarrassment for the both of you. Be sure to explain that you wouldn't recommend her reading it because it has far too many "steamy" parts. Or you might say that there are lots of "love scenes," but they are "too graphic" for your own tastes. Tell her that the way "society" is today, there is no wonder that a book like this has become so popular (again, old people also LOVE to discuss this). You could also tell her that you learned all about the books from reading articles about them and watching the news, not from reading them. Whatever you do, don't tell her that you have all three books and that you were in a *Fifty Shades* book club. And should the subject come up again in her presence, always say with sincerest indignation, "*Fifty Shades*? Are people still talking about that garbage?!"

• •

> **WRITE notes about, annotate, or underline the places in this essay in which the author makes assumptions about elderly women, such as the indications that one would need to "modify the potentially offensive parts" and her advice to "emphasize that Anna reforms Christian, the two get married, and start a family." Next, organize your annotations into themes. Possible themes might include "octogenarians are out of touch" and "octogenarian women don't like or appreciate sexual content." Finally, create a possible outline for a rhetorical analysis of "How to Explain *Fifty Shades of Gray* to an Octogenarian" that has as its thesis: "How to Explain *Fifty Shades of Gray* to an Octogenarian" reveals as much about the author's perceptions of elderly women as it does how to describe *Fifty Shades* to them.**

• •

Argument

An Introduction to Writing Argument

Leslie Reed

Argument. This word carries a negative connotation for many people. When they hear the word argument, they often think of an unpleasant screaming match, and this is certainly one definition of argument. In fact, the first definition of argument that comes up on Google is, "an exchange of diverging or opposite views, typically a heated or angry one." The idea of people angrily fighting about something, possibly hurling insults at each other, is right there in the definition. Most people do not enjoy engaging in this sort of activity or even being present when it is occurring so no wonder so many students have negative reactions to the term. Luckily, argument has a definition other than that of a vicious quarrel. The second Google definition of argument is one that applies to more lofty (and academic) pursuits, argument as "a reason or set of reasons given with the aim of persuading others that an action or idea is right or wrong." This definition has its roots in the ancient Greek philosophers and their concept of argument, especially Aristotle's *The Art of Rhetoric*. In his writings, Aristotle defined rules of argument and explained how rhetorical appeals persuade audiences. This idea of argument, one of using reason to persuade, is our goal when writing an argumentative essay—an essay in which the author seeks to convince the audience that his or her unique claim is right and does so with integrity.

It is important to note here that if everyone agrees upon an issue, there is no one left to persuade, which is how a researched argument essay is different than a research paper or report, genres that attempt to objectively present facts about a subject. A researched argument also considers and presents the findings, theories, and opinions of experts, but uses the information to create a unique claim.

To many students, writing an argumentative essay seems intimidating because they feel that they do not have the ability to add their perspective to an issue. However, did you know that you have been making and supporting your own claims for most of your life? Allow me to explain. Have you ever experienced a situation where two friends in a quarrel each wanted you to agree with his or her argument, yet you refused to take sides? Perhaps, when you were asked, you explained that you did not fully agree with either friend and offered your explanation about why you partially disagreed (or agreed) with both? If you have done this, or have ever provided your own solution to a problem someone was facing, you have presented and supported your own distinctive claim. A major difference is that you will likely not be writing about your friends or your own life directly, though topics about which you have a personal stake are typically going to result in better, more engaging papers. You will also not be talking to your friends in this paper, but instead you will be writing to an unseen audience, which means you will have to carefully explain your reasoning and evidence and define key terms so that your readers will be able to follow and fully understand your perspective and the progression of your essay.

In order to transfer your argumentative skills from the context of a verbal conversation to one that takes place on paper, you should think of the argumentative essay just as you do a spoken conversation. When you are speaking to someone else, you do not want to repeat something that someone has already said. Instead, you should listen until you have something new to contribute. In order to "listen" to others when beginning a researched argument, students should begin with the research. You may have an idea about the claim you are going to make, and that's fine, but begin by reading— or listening—to what others are saying about the subject. Then, just like in a conversation, you can decide when and how best to respond.

The most important part of your response is that it belongs to you. There are many controversial issues that have been around for so long that everyone seems to know both sides of the argument, and while it is fine to agree with either one of those sides, you would not want to use someone else's argument as your response. When issues are closely examined, we often find that there are much more useful and interesting ways to argue than with an either/or position. Before you settle on a topic, ask yourself the following questions: Why is this topic one I should weigh in on? What do I already know about this topic and what do I need to know before making an educated argument? What is my argument? How is my argument different that others I've read? What will my readers need to know in order to be persuaded by me? What arguments can I anticipate from people who will disagree with me and how can I frame my responses to their arguments in ways that will persuade them to agree with me or at least respect my argument? How will I best present this information to them?

Contributing new ideas to the conversation can seem hard to accomplish at first glance, but as you read your sources, you will find that you actually do have something to say. And remember, that is the point of this assignment: to help you learn to communicate and support your claim and have others see the reasoning that supports your point of view. To this end, the section to follow provides various examples and genres of argumentative essays. Your instructor may use these essays in class to help you learn the different characteristics of this genre and the rhetorical choices you have to make when you compose them.

Argument

• •

WRITE responses to the following questions to help generate issues about which you might argue.

• •

- The latest debate or scandal you've heard or read about?
- Most recent article you read?
- Look at a newspaper's website or its front page. Which story is of the most interest to you?
- Something you know more about than the average person?
- Something you've learned more about in the last month?
- The last thing you saw or read that made you angry?
- Something going on in the news that you don't quite understand?
- Favorite hobby? A topic of debate in your favorite hobby?
- Top 2 College courses you've taken? Favorite discussions or topics of debate from these courses?
- A debate in your field of study/major?
- An issue you've made up your mind about?
- An issue about which you have not yet made up your mind?
- Something you want to change about the university?
- Something you want to change about your community?
- Something you want to change about the world?

CORBIN EDWARDS

Corbin Edwards—20, 5'10", Caucasian, blonde, blue-green eyes, 135 lbs., Little Rock. Can be seen wearing glasses, shirts found at thrift stores or deep within the attic, joggers, tube socks, and the infamous bird-patterned five-panel hat. Keeps a cheap Neff watch on his boney wrist and falls short keeping high-quality street aesthetic. Currently single. Earbuds are glued unless during conversation. Daydreams about best possible life outcomes are ever-present over the sound of underground hip-hop. Borderline theist. Interests include starting and never finishing FL Studio beats, playing Runescape, and lighting gasoline-saturated pumpkins on fire in dark parking lots. Two years at A-State, computer science major, a handful of friends plus a couple of enemies. Number of programming contests participated—2. Number of Tinder matches this month—0. Occasionally writes music reviews, sappy poetry, and free-form, grammatically incorrect autobiographies for fun. Non-music or uninteresting writing assignments are typically tackled with crass procrastination.[1]

THE ASSIGNMENT: JUSTIFYING AN EVALUATION

An evaluative argument is an essay that asks authors to make a judgment or evaluation of the value, meaning, or quality of a subject of their choosing. This evaluation should be based on the author's own reasoning and interpretation. Authors should be careful to state their judgment and the reasons behind it in a thesis and to support their reasons with specific examples. They should also consider objections or alternatives to this judgment and explain why their evaluation is valid nonetheless. The assignment also requires the use of researched sources that should serve as support for the thesis and be cited in the appropriate style.

Note: In the middle of the first paragraph, you will see a rather long in-text citation. Though it may seem strange at first glance, scholars often list two or more sources in the same parenthetical citation if those sources are both quoted in the same sentence, contain similar information, or can be used to support one another. The resulting in-text reference is called a citation string. To create a citation string in MLA format, list the in-text citation information for each source that is referenced in the order it is mentioned in the text, and separate each entry with a semicolon. If the sources are not referenced in the sentence, place them in alphabetical order. Also note that Corbin opted to use Kendrick Lamar's intended capitalization and punctuation when referencing Lamar's album, good kid, m.A.A.d city. How does this choice add or detract from Corbin's ethos?

---

1   Note that Corbin chose to write his own bio. See page 75 for a prompt to help you do the same.

A Benchmark in Hip Hop

Corbin Edwards

Written for Marcus Tribbett's Honors Composition I Course
. . . .

"A war that was based on apartheid and discrimination made me wanna go back to the city and tell the homies what I learned. The word was respect."

—Kendrick Lamar

To Pimp a Butterfly is the third full-length album released by Kendrick Lamar, a rapper who hails from the streets of Compton in Los Angeles, California. Lamar gave only a couple of weeks' notice before dropping the album in March 2015. The bar was set high for the new album after the critical acclaim his platinum album *good kid, m.A.A.d city* received. Despite selling slightly less than *good kid*, *To Pimp a Butterfly* was awarded a better overall Metacritic score and more 10/10s from critics ("good kid…"; "To Pimp…"). Some critics, like Anthony Fantano from *The Needle Drop*, believe *To Pimp a Butterfly* "could possibly be the best rap record of the decade" and that Lamar "signifies a new chapter" in hip hop (Fantano 21:09 and 21:27). *To Pimp a Butterfly* is one of the most important albums of the decade so far because of its interesting music, message, and present impact upon society.

To Pimp a Butterfly's phenomenal music presents itself in a rich manner. Unlike many popular trap rap records from the past five years, this album gathers its influences from jazz, soul, and funk. At the beginning of "For Free?" a sexy saxophone solo and a wall of gospel choir instantly meet the listener. Then a sassy black woman yells at someone over a frantic drum beat layered under sporadic piano playing. "King Kunta" features funky female backup vocalists repeating almost every bar Lamar throws, all over a groovy bass line that makes head bobbing easy. A small soul group sings the hook in "Complexion (Zulu Love)" who also provide nice counter melodies as Lamar raps. Lamar himself keeps the album interesting by introducing many unique voices. In "Hood Politics," he sounds almost like a nasally child, while in "The Blacker the Berry," the listener can hear the wrath in his hard-hitting delivery. He even goes as far as to impersonate his momma in "You Ain't Gotta Lie (Momma Said)." The album's amazing composition features many pleasant flows and musical transitions. "Institutionalized" creates a musical shift at the one minute mark of the song, as Lamar switches from high-pitched rapping along a lo-fi instrumental to half singing, half rapping over a more traditional hip hop beat.

The second act of "Institutionalized" also features a miniature story told by Snoop Dogg and an oddly catchy hook sung by Bilal impersonating a grandmother. The first half of "u" presents angry Lamar repeating "Lovin' you is complicated" over a crazy jazz session, transitioning to a more melancholy scene; the listener gets pushed onto the floor of a hotel room as a drunken Lamar cries a spoken word poem about his regrets, bottles clinking in the background (Lamar). The music in the album goes against the flow of current mainstream rap by reverting back to the genre's jazz and soul roots.

To Pimp a Butterfly may just be as symbolically rich as it is musically. The album contains many different themes and messages that skew the usual hip hop themes of sex, money, and drugs. As Jude Clarke from *Drowned in Sound* states, "*To Pimp a Butterfly* is a concept album with many themes, which interlock and overlap. It isn't a straight narrative, instead leaving the listener to fill in some of the gaps for herself." An illustration of this is "Mortal Man," which closes the album with a poem, spoken by Lamar to Tupac, explaining the meaning behind the album. Lamar's rise out of Compton is like the metamorphosis of a butterfly, hence the title of the album.

Unlike most rappers who seem to celebrate "making it out" of their rough neighborhoods through the indulgence of sex and drugs, Lamar doesn't really celebrate at all. In fact, he uses his fame to try to speak out against the crime in his streets. "The Blacker the Berry" seems like a hateful message towards white people, but is actually a satirical piece towards narrow-minded gang bangers. Lines like "You made me a killer" and "So why did I weep when Trayvon Martin was in the street? When gang banging make me kill a nigga blacker than me? Hypocrite!" satirize the hypocrisy of people who destroy their own communities in order to rebel against a cause they may find racist (Lamar). Lamar speaks against victimization, implying it's not the key to winning. People have to work hard to build a good reputation, as the grandma in "Institutionalized" sings (Lamar). The messages on this album are broad and serious yet personal and compelling. As Fantano points out, Lamar isn't "delivering some sort of re-blogged, 140 character, bumper sticker philosophy" (Fantano 11:54).

To Pimp a Butterfly's importance not only comes from its unique musical styles and powerful messages, it also branches from the people who listen to it. The current decade has housed controversies over police brutality, like with the death of Eric Garner. As the problem of racist police brutality gets more coverage in the media, many African-Americans feel mistreated and segregated, which sparks events like the Ferguson riots. Kendrick Lamar's messages in *To Pimp a Butterfly* fit nicely with the

current controversies, so his voice is easily heard in America. His impact is evidenced by an event that happened only four months after the album's release. A group of activists at Cleveland University protested police brutality by chanting, "We gonna be alright!" ("Activists chant..."), which is the chorus from the most popular song on *To Pimp a Butterfly*, "Alright." Lamar has clearly inspired people to fight for their rights in an appropriate way, instead of violently and ignorantly.

Lamar has also influenced hip hop as a whole. He has made many features on many different rap songs as well as appearing in a remix of Taylor Swift's "Bad Blood." He also helped write Dr. Dre's newest album, *Compton* (Navjosh), the first release from the hip hop billionaire since 2001, and has gained massive critical acclaim for *good kid, m.A.A.d city* and *To Pimp a Butterfly* (Metacritic). Together with Lamar's impressive resume and sending the right message at the right time, *To Pimp a Butterfly* has slowly started to impact society and will continue to do so as long as unwarranted violence affects black culture.

To Pimp a Butterfly houses fantastic music and powerful messages through its theatrical imagery, as well as causing a positive ripple in black communities across the country. Very few critics gave the album a negative review, which leaves most of the negativity to casual listeners. Some listeners might be turned off by the album because it's not as trendy as *good kid, m.A.A.d city*, but one has to understand that the album's music is inspired by old school hip hop, jazz, and funk. One critical review in particular doesn't like the influences and reads, "The jazz sections are purposely chaotic but lack symmetry" (Doc Zeus). I disagree with this review because even though the jazz isn't as pristine as the works of John Coltrane, it serves its purpose to uphold the chaos of the ghetto—twisted, dirty, and imperfect. The album modernizes its influences in Lamar's own intricate way. Some people may think some messages in the album encourage victimization and white hate. Yet, if the ongoing poem read by Lamar in every song is analyzed properly, one can make the connections to the themes in each song and realize that Lamar desires unification. The impact the album makes on society may seem blurry as of 2015, but the fact that people chanted "Alright" at protests only a few months after the album's release seems positive for the album's future solidity. I believe *To Pimp a Butterfly* will eventually undergo a metamorphosis like its title. Some people don't understand its importance now, but in a few years' time the sun will glisten off its wings as it changes the streets.

Works Cited

"Activists Chant Kendrick Lamar's Alright during Police Harassment Protest." *Guardian News and Media Limited*, 29 July 2015, www.theguardian.com/music/2015/jul/29/activists-chant-kendrick-lamar-track-alright-police-harassment-protests.

Clarke, Jude. "Album Review: Kendrick Lamar—To Pimp a Butterfly." *Drowned In Sound*, 23 Mar. 2015, drownedinsound.com/releases/18771/reviews/4148937.

Doc Zeus. "Guns and Butterflies: The Complications of Kendrick Lamar's Sophomore Album." *Passion of the Weiss*, Passion of the Weiss LLC, 20 Mar. 2015, www.passionweiss.com/2015/03/20/kendrick-lamar-to-pimp-a-butterfly-review/.

Fantano, Anthony. "Kendrick Lamar—To Pimp a Butterfly Album Review." *YouTube*, uploaded by The Needle Drop, 18 March 2015, www.youtube.com/watch?v=qTmHuavOXNg.

"*good kid, m.A.A.d city* by Kendrick Lamar." *Metacritic*. CBS Interactive Inc., www.metacritic.com/music/good-kid-maad-city/kendrick-lamar. Accessed 21 Oct. 2015.

Lamar, Kendrick. *To Pimp a Butterfly*, Interscope Records, 2015.

Navjosh. "Dr. Dre—'Compton: A Soundtrack' (Full Credits / Booklet Scans)." *HipHopNMore*. HipHop-N-More, 21 Aug. 2015, hiphop-n-more.com/2015/08/dr-dre-compton-a-soundtrack-full-credits/. Accessed 21 Oct. 2015.

"To Pimp A Butterfly by Kendrick Lamar." *Metacritic*. CBS Interactive Inc., www.metacritic.com/music/to-pimp-a-butterfly/kendrick-lamar. Accessed 21 Oct. 2015.

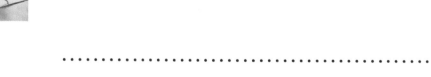

• •

Note: When inputting URLs in MLA 8 you use the entire web address, with the exception of "http://."

• •

Argument

Note: Corbin Edwards opted to write his own biographical statement. What do you think of it? Do you think all of the bios in this collection should be like Corbin's? Why or why not? As you read it, consider and make assumptions about who he is and what he's like not only based on what he says, but how he says it. This exercise will help you prepare for this short writing exercise:

WRITE a short biographical statement about yourself that illustrates who you are and what you're like not just in what you say, but how you say it. For example, if you are quiet and reserved, consider how you might convey this in your tone. If you are extroverted and adventurous, allow these traits to be reflected in your style and organization.

BETHANY GALLIMORE

Bethany Gallimore, English Major and A-State graduate student, is a strong proponent of the writing process, arguing that her best writing is usually done through the process of long hours and many drafts. She credits Composition I and II as further aiding her development as a writer, noting that "Since taking Composition I and II, I have learned to streamline my writing process, but the 'think, write, rewrite, edit' formula is still my go-to for important projects."

Her advice to Composition I and II students? "Students should take notes! You may not have that one spark of inspiration again. So, jot down ideas while in class, scribble on the margins of your book, and get those ideas out and on paper."

THE ASSIGNMENT: PROPOSING A SOLUTION PAPER

Many discussions about contested issues are problem-focused. This is particularly evident in the news media, but it's also evident in some scholarship. Effective solution papers, however, not only identify and define a problem fully, but they also describe a solution clearly. Additionally, effective solution papers will make it clear to the readers why they should care about this issue and how they can partake in the solution.

For this assignment, you will define a problem of particular interest or importance to you and argue for a specific solution, giving examples to make the problem specific and relatable to your audience. These examples might include startling statistics, scenarios or anecdotes to dramatize the problem, and testimony from those affected by the problem. You will also want to incorporate credible sources and counter-argument to establish your credibility as an authority on the subject and substantiate your argument.

Photo courtesy of Caitlin Lafarlette

Our Planet, Our Plastic, and Our Problem: A Personal Approach to Reducing Plastic Waste

Bethany Gallimore

Written for Marcus Tribbett's Composition I Course

Argument

As I begin my essay, I lounge in the Student Union and slowly allow my brain to be numbed by the sheer volume of plastic waste research. *This is just terrible*, I think. I silently berate the hundreds of thousands of Americans too addicted to their own convenient lifestyles to care about the 73 thousand tons of plastic they discard every day (Burns "What to Do"). *Shame on them.* I drain the last of my Starbucks caramel mocha as I set my pen back on the table. *Mmm, so good.* It is at this moment I realize I am the problem. What am I doing? My hypocrisy slaps me across the face. Isn't this the epitome of first-world consumerism—a single serving of coffee elegantly presented in an earth-killing container? The plastic to-go lid will last far longer than my short-lived dose of overpriced caffeine and sugar. Even the more biodegradable cardboard cup supports a thin inner lining of plastic. I have been researching plastic waste for weeks, yet I still act as though the care of Earth lies in the hands of others. But I am wrong. I am responsible for my lifestyle. This is my planet, this is my plastic, and this is my problem.

The problem is not that we are using plastic, it is that we are using too much. Synthetic plastic has increased in use on an exponential scale since its inception in 1909 (Doucette). When the polymer first gained popularity it was heralded as the savior of natural resources, the magic pill for the productivity of society, and the overarching solution for cheaper and more sustainable materials worldwide (Hohn 61). But no developer could have predicted the extent to which plastic would permeate society. Plastics can now be used for nearly any purpose from coat hangers and computer drives to M&M packages and medical equipment, and it is their seemingly infinite possibilities that allow plastics to keep a stranglehold on society. "Annual plastic consumption worldwide has increased from five million tons in the 1950s to around 280 million tons today," writes Marino Xanthos of the *Korea Times*. The global production of plastic tops one million pounds per minute, and half of that will go to single-use disposable products (*Bag It*; Xanthos). The miracle pill has proved far from miraculous though as overconsumption threatens to deplete fossil fuel reserves, choke the oceans with thousands of miles of garbage patches, and pose serious health threats to millions of people worldwide.

The common synthetic polymers known as plastics are derivatives of petroleum, a fossil fuel compacted beneath the earth's crust over thousands of years. Through an extensive polymerization process of addition and condensation reactions, the refined petroleum attains the familiar shapes of Coke bottles, coat buttons, and calculator backings (Burns "Polymers"). The United States alone devotes 17 million barrels of oil each year to the production of plastic material. Some environmentalists say as little as forty years' worth of fossil fuel now remains, if the current consumption trajectory is unchanged (*Bag It*). Disputes arise not when these irreplaceable resources are devoted to plastics, but when those resources are carelessly thrown away. "Petroleum is way too important and way too scarce to us to throw away like this," says environmental scientist Richard Conlin (*Bag It*).

I glare at my now-empty coffee cup, wondering just how much oil went into its creation. I lean back in my chair and ponder the life my disposable cup will lead after it leaves my hands. This single cup will soon be just one more piece of the 27 million tons of plastic discarded each year (Burns "What to Do"). In fact, most plastic waste will find an eventual home in the oceanic realm, according to Doucette. Over 7 million tons of garbage enter the oceans every year, and once the waste gets in, it is nearly impossible to take back out (Karpus 67). Bottle tops, diaper bags, milk jugs and more slowly swirl into murky concentric heaps called gyres, known in uncomforting layman's terms simply as garbage patches. These garbage patches can encompass up to half a million acres and extend hundreds of feet below surface level (Doucette). Far from being floating "islands" of intact bath toys, 18-ounce drink cups, and to-go boxes, the plastic in the garbage patches is broken down by a combination of sunlight and salt water into a thick soup of micro particles (Kostigen). In some parts of the Pacific Ocean, these micro particles outweigh zooplankton by a margin of 6 to 1, causing critical levels of plastic ingestion in whales, sea birds, and fish, as well as in the plankton themselves (Kostigen; Doucette). Scientists estimate that as many as 100,000 marine animals die each year from plastic ingestion, the majority of those being adolescent or immature at the time of death (*Bag It*).

So why should I care? I stare moodily at my now inkless red plastic pen that will soon meet the same fate as its coffee cup counterpart. *It's the ocean. The ocean can take it.* But it may not be able to for much longer. Pollution-caused deaths contribute to species declination and eventual extinction, which could make vulnerable the entire oceanic ecosystem (*The 11th Hour*). In addition, as much as a third of the world's population relies on fish for 20 percent of the animal protein in their diet, so polluted fish could mean polluted humans (Kostigen). Ingestion of the chemical byproduct BPA is also on the forefront of the plastic use controversy, having been linked to deformities and health problems among animals and people.

The problem with this picture is that most people do not realize the effect their plastic waste has on the environment and other humans, and the few who do know often do not care to change their lifestyle. According to Banbury, Stinerock, and Subrahmanyan, "(C)consumers often fail to make the connection between elements of their consumption behavior and elements of the sustainability agenda." Most people see the problem of overconsumption as something to which they do not contribute. I look back down at my lap, slightly more somber, and run my finger over the plastic rim of the to-go cup. *Okay, so I have a problem. I'm careless with my plastic, but what can I do about it?* I recall the now-familiar adage: reduce, reuse, and recycle.

Aha! Problem solved! It's recyclable! The triangular symbol etched into the surface proudly proclaims my container to be a number six recyclable product. *See? I'm not a bad person. Recycling saves the earth.* Unfortunately though, in reality, only about five percent of plastic products are recycled, and recycling can be a labor and waste intensive process (Hohn 61). The number six polystyrene plastics are actually the second lowest score on the list with only a 0.8 percent recycling rate, coming just in front of number three vinyl and PVC products which score at nearly zero (*Bag It*). The number one polyethylene terephthalates—plastic bottles, milk jugs, and food storage containers—rate the highest, but still only manage to be recycled at a rate of around 20 percent (Burns "What to Do;" *Bag It*). In addition, the number ones are most usually "down-cycled" into inferior quality plastids, which are unable to reenter to recycling process (*Bag It*).

Unsatisfactory recycling ratios are not the only problem faced in elevating recycling as the sole solution to the proliferation of unwanted plastic. Although the triune self-chasing arrows form a nationally recognized symbol, regulation of this symbol is nonexistent and allows pools of truly recyclable material to be contaminated with tainted products (*Bag It*). The premise of recycling plastic waste is a hopeful sounding option and can drastically reduce the effect humans have on the planet, but it is not quite the panacea consumers have been led to believe. "By offering the false promise of disposability, of consumption without cost, it has helped create a culture of wasteful make-believe, an economy of forgetting" (Hohn 61). This statement helps further illustrate that people do forget, they do neglect to think about their actions, and they do avoid personal sacrifice in the face of more convenient-sounding options.

But if recycling doesn't work, what do I do with this cup? My mind wanders back to the second word in the popular catchphrase: reuse. *Well, I guess I can get another serving from it.* I doubtfully glance at the cardboard exterior. Though my coffee cup may not be the best candidate for continuous reuse, many common plastic products are. If one person repurposed all of their plastic 18-ounce soda bottles for water usage instead of purchasing virgin material water bottles, they could prevent thousands of pounds of plastic refuse from entering the environment just over the course of a single year. Even major corporations are beginning to recognize the opportunities reuse offers. In Germany, beverage companies have installed public plastic bottle deposit kiosks in which customers can return their used drink bottles in exchange for a monetary voucher. But instead of undergoing the extensive recycling process, these bottles are directly reincorporated into the soda distribution industry, eliminating the need for expensive remolding procedures (*Bag It*).

Although not what one would initially consider a part of the reuse umbrella, incineration is another surprisingly promising option for reaping the maximum benefit from discarded plastics. Pure plastic can produce twice the energy gained from burning coal, offering a doubly beneficial environmental choice (Burns "What to Do"). While simply burning plastic releases harmful carbon based air toxins, incineration—burning the plastics at extremely high temperatures—prevents the toxins from entering the atmosphere ("Making Stuff: Cleaner"). In addition, the ash from the incinerators can be repurposed and used to pave roads, make cinderblocks, and even create artificial reefs for displaced marine life (Burns "What to Do").

So I stretch in the oversized red chair, quite relieved to be reaching the end of my research. *Good problem solving. Kudos to me.* But the thought creeps in, even these promising solutions would not have to be initiated if we as consumers would follow the first part of the three-pronged sustainability design and simply reduce. Reduce the amount of plastic shopping bags we use, reduce the over-packaging we acquire from retailers, reduce the wasteful discarding of valuable reusable materials, and reduce the apathy so prevalent throughout our first-world culture. The only thing we need to increase is awareness, awareness that the problem of plastic waste exists, that we are the people causing it, and that we are also responsible for dealing with the results of our actions. Now we face a choice. We can leave our chairs, clap politely, and toss the Starbuck's cup into the plastic garbage bin on the way out the doors. Or, we can stand, owning up to our actions and refusing to continue as we have. I silently ponder my own question, then gently place the cold, dry cup into my denim backpack. It will still be good for another few trips. Then I can switch to the Red Wolf graduation mug that so far has seen far too little action. I may not be able to change my past actions, but I can control my future. This is my world, and plastic waste is my problem. Is it yours?

Argument

Works Cited

The 11th Hour. Directed by Nadia Conners and Leila Conners Petersen. Produced and narrated by Leonardo DiCaprio, Warner Independent Pictures, 2007.

Bag It. Directed by Suzan Beraza. Performance by Jeb Berrier, Real Thing Films, 2010.

Banbury, Catherine, et al. "Sustainable Consumption: Introspecting Across Multiple Lived Cultures." *Journal of Business Research*, vol. 65, no. 4, 2012, pp. 497–503. *ScienceDirect*, www.sciencedirect.com/science/article/pii/S0148296311000610.

Burns, Katherine. "Polymers." Physical Science, 25 March 2013, Arkansas State University, Jonesboro. Lecture.

---. "What to Do With Plastic Waste?" Physical Science, 27 March 2013, Arkansas State University, Jonesboro. Lecture.

Doucette, Kitt. "An Ocean of Plastic." *Rolling Stone*, vol. 1090, 29 Oct. 2009, p. 54, *MasterFILE Premier*, eds.a.ebscohost.com/ehost/detail/detail?vid=2&sid=d9ce0722-7750-4a69-ba28-c2381010f266%40sessionmgr4007&hid=4108&bdata=JnNpdGU9ZWhvc3QtbGl2ZQ%3d%3d#AN=44760762&db=f5h.

Hohn, Donovan. "Moby-Duck, or, the Synthetic Wilderness of Childhood." *Harper's Magazine*, Jan. 2007, harpers.org/archive/2007/01/moby-duck/.

Karpus, Leah. "Plastic in Our Oceans." *Alive: Canada's Natural Health & Wellness Magazine*, vol. 355, May 2012, pp. 66–71, *Consumer Health Complete—EBSCOhost*, eds.b.ebscohost.com/eds/pdfviewer/pdfviewer?vid=1&sid=c7a508fd-5f4c-459f-8c8f-9d050ee9bdf9%40sessionmgr104&hid=108.

Kostigen, Thomas M. "Better Planet Garbage Patch." *Discover*, vol. 29, no. 7, 2008, pp. 24–26, *Academic Search Ultimate*, eds.a.ebscohost.com/ehost/detail/detail?vid=2&sid=fb4ec201-a3a3-4a1a-9b9f-f62017a5b434%40sessionmgr4007&hid=4108&bdata=JnNpdGU9ZWhvc3QtbGl2ZQ%3d%3d#AN=32580464&db=asn.

"Making Stuff: Cleaner." created by NOVA, performance by David Pogue, *PBS Online*, 01 Feb. 2011, www.pbs.org/video/1768954299/.

Xanthos, Marino. "The Dirt on Plastic Waste." *Korea Times*, 17 Mar. 2013, www.koreatimes.co.kr/www/news/opinon/2016/07/197_132235.html.

MOHAMMED GHIAS

Mohammed loves knowledge, and believes it is the most powerful tool a person can possess as it is always stored in one's mind, and one can never deplete it, lose it, or have it taken from him or her. In order to learn anything and be successful in it, Mohammed believes that one must not only have a passion for the knowledge one might gain, but also for the love and kindness that the person will spread by helping others through employing that knowledge. For this reason, Mohammed will continue his education and pursue a doctorate in the future.

By bringing aspects of his personal life into the paper titled "Monsters," Mohammed tries to connect with and intrigue his readers. This is because he believes that every person has similar feelings, but some are more sensitive to certain feelings, and others are more adept at hiding them, only to get haunted by them later. If there is something that a person can relate to or that evokes certain feelings, he or she will become more interested in that medium. Connecting to people is the most important step to get one's points across and make them understandable and interesting. This was the logic used behind "Monsters."

THE ASSIGNMENT: EXTENDED DEFINITION ESSAY

The Extended Definition essay is a specific type of argumentative essay in which the author advances a particular meaning that he or she believes can or should define a concept. This meaning is usually explained or illustrated through pointing out how the concept is similar to what people may already know or understand about it, adding to it a set of characteristics that are unique to the author's interpretation of that concept.

Because the best place to begin this essay is with something familiar to the audience, authors often lead with a logical definition of the concept that is commonly accepted or understood. The key, however, is to then expand or extend the accepted perception of that concept. As with other argumentative essays, an Extended Definition will usually discuss a subject which holds significance or interest to the author or reader; as such, this essay can define any concept on any subject ranging from politics to pop culture, or anywhere in between. It is important that the author expresses a specific, clear interpretation of the concept that adds to or changes the logical (dictionary) definition and makes his or her views stronger by supporting them with researched evidence. Research in support of the author's opinion or argument only helps strengthen the validity of the extended definition. Authors should also take care to investigate and discuss the views which oppose his or her argument, as this will foster a solid ethos for him or her which will allow the reader to judge the strength and application of the author's definition in real situations.

Monstrosity

Mohammed Ghias

Written for Kerri Bennett's Composition II Course
. . . .

"There are no such things as monsters!" This saying has been repeated to us several times during childhood. We were all terrified of a grossly malformed creature coming out of the dark closet at night and eating us. Now that we are adults, we have realized that monsters do not actually exist. However, our fear of monsters has not gone away. We still worry that something unusual could happen any time to disrupt our smooth and routine lifestyle. A monstrosity is something that is out of the norm of society, something that is unfamiliar to human nature and our beliefs in a way that touches our unusual instincts and evokes fear.

Most humans are accustomed to a structured, smooth lifestyle. When something threatens our comfortable lifestyles and poses unanticipated challenges, we are forced to leave our comfort zones and explore the intimidating boundaries of our lives. The thing that interferes could be real, such as a person or a creature, or it could be imaginary. These things are what we consider to be monstrous. Both types of monsters, real and imaginary, are dangerous. With real monsters, we can analyze their faces before they attack, and therefore, escape. As Allen Gervaise writes, "facial expressions are considered as communicative signals: they are central features of social behavior of most nonhuman primates and they are powerful stimuli in human communication" (31). We are biologically hardwired to see and analyze the facial expressions of living things so that we can recognize which person or creature could be a potential threat. In contrast, imaginary monsters are more difficult to escape from, since they only exist in our human minds.

We often explore these fears through film. For example, in zombie movies people are often forced to depart from their usual routines of life in order to survive the apocalypse. If this were to happen in reality this break with routine lifestyles and uncommon behavior would cause great fear because it is something very uncommon to human nature. The people forced to leave their day-to-day activities due to a zombie apocalypse initially react with confusion, which causes panic. The second source of fear comes from the zombies' facial expressions, which certainly appear as a potential threat to the safety of the human race. This same threat can exist among humans also.

The nature of fictional monsters exists in the human mind. The depiction of fictional monsters with cannibalistic properties, such as zombies, vampires, and werewolves, are often attributed to Countess Elizabeth Bathory; a woman who was "accused of torturing young women, tearing the flesh from their living bodies with her teeth and bathing in their blood in her quest for eternal youth" (Kürti, 136). This shows that the behaviors of most monsters in fictional stories are actually derived from the innate natures and thoughts of humans. For instance, a kidnapper, who is a human, is also considered a monster. This is because the family of the victim must disrupt its usual lifestyle to deal with the police and usually the intimidating ransom phone calls from the kidnapper. The kidnapped person also has to face the kidnapper, and has to see his or her monstrous facial expressions, which must be threatening.

Another example of a fictional monster with horrible behaviors is the werewolf. Werewolves, as described by Nathan Moses Szanjnberg, are normal humans, except on a full-moon night when they go under transformation, which is an uncontrollable process, and hunt humans for dinner (899). This fictional monster, also based on the human Bathory, has intimidating features. Humans are naturally afraid of the dark, and are especially afraid of creatures that kill and eat them. Since werewolves come out at night and eat humans, it seems apparent that the creature was invented by the human mind to embody the greatest fears that we find within ourselves.

Although fear is caused by monstrosity; this monstrosity does not have to be real. According to Gervaise, a person may consider an entity or a situation dangerous for him/her, even though it may not really be the case (114). Fear is our innate, biological emotion that is necessary to protect us from danger. However, if a person is feeling fearful in a situation that is not deemed by society to be dangerous, what is the person really afraid of? People that have anxiety disorders have irrational fears, which seems like they are battling an imaginary, dark monster that is hard or impossible to defeat.

Fear caused by monstrosity is our natural mechanism for protecting ourselves and escaping from dangers. Monstrosity can be real or imaginary. A real monster, which can be a human, disrupts our smooth lifestyle, forcing us to leave our comfort zones. On the other hand, imaginary monsters attack us in the form of anxiety disorders. These imaginary monsters can last for a long time, as they cannot be seen and force us to explore outside our comfort zones. Fear is the inevitable result of this. Fictional monsters do not exist, but are based on humans. This means that the nature and behaviors of fictional monsters are based on human instincts. A society must strive to eradicate monstrosity in order to reach maximum productivity and to prevent future human monsters.

Works Cited

Gervaise, Allen D. *Psychology of Emotions, Motivations and Actions: Psychology of Fear.* Nova Science Publishers, 2012.

Kürti, László. "The Symbolic Construction Of The Monstrous—The Elizabeth Bathory Story." *Narodna umjetnost: Croatian Journal of Ethnology and Folklore Research*, 2009, pp. 133–159.

Szajnberg, Nathan Moses. "Zombies, Vampires, Werewolves: An Adolescent's Developmental System For The Undead And Their Ambivalent Dependence On The Living, And Technical Implications." *Psychoanalytic Review*, vol. 99, no. 6, 2012, pp. 897–910.

Argument

CONNOR PATROM

Connor Patrom was raised in the small town of Beebe, Arkansas. It was there that he attended Beebe Public Schools. During his high school career, Connor played many sports and took pride in achieving academic excellence. He graduated from Beebe High School with honors in 2016.

After high school, Connor started to attend Arkansas State University. His plan was to obtain a civil engineering degree, but he soon learned that he liked working with people instead of numbers. He is now on track to obtain a Bachelor's degree in Communication Disorders with hopes of becoming a speech-language pathologist. As a sophomore, Connor has continued his academic achievements by making it on the Dean's List.

THE ASSIGNMENT: ARGUMENTATIVE ESSAY

An argumentative essay usually directly responds to an issue of cultural or personal significance or importance to the author or reader. These papers can cover anything from local or national politics, views on pop culture, or an issue that is currently in public discussion. It is important that the author takes a specific, clear stand on the issue and makes his or her views stronger by supporting it with concrete or specific examples.

Authors should also investigate and discuss the opposing viewpoint of his or her own position, as this will bring clarity and a well-roundedness to the paper that allows the reader to judge the strength of the author's position in regards to the factual and practical aspects of the issue. Depending upon the assignment, this essay may also require some outside research and cited sources.

To Vote or Not to Vote

Connor Patrom

Written for Haley Fitzgerald's Composition I Course

• •

During the upcoming election, the options the American people have for the position of President of the United States both have views that go against the entirety of my morals and values. I feel as if this election is choosing the "lesser of two evils" and I can honestly say that I cannot make that choice. Even if it is our right to vote, the wrongdoings of Donald Trump and Hillary Clinton are pushing me to choose not to vote in the 2016 Presidential election.

Hillary Clinton is known throughout America for the liberal views she holds and the lies she has told. It is for these reasons that I couldn't vote for this woman. I respect Hillary Clinton in that she is the first woman to win a presidential nomination and is paving the road for women in America, but there is one topic that she holds a strong view on. Abortion. Clinton thinks that abortion is a woman's right and that it should be legal everywhere. If she became our next president, it would certainly be that way. I believe that abortion is morally wrong and it does not matter where it takes place in a woman's pregnancy. Clinton also wants to put an end to the American people's right to own firearms. It is in fact true that robberies and deaths involving firearms are higher than in years past, but this will not stop even if she tries to end it. People who want to kill another human being can find ways to obtain a firearm, just like locking the door of your house will not keep a criminal out, they will simply find another way in. There are always ways around government restrictions and criminals would find ways to exploit them, so why take out a way for law-abiding American citizens to protect themselves? Hillary Clinton is also a liar. She lied about the 33,000 emails she deleted and to the families who grieved regarding Benghazi. Everybody lies, but to continue to claim innocence even after being proved wrong shows a strong lack of character. I can't force myself to vote for a woman that could potentially put the American people in harm's way.

Donald Trump is a name known not only in America, but around the world and in no way is he better than Hillary Clinton. Trump is a very well-known business man, yet he has no political background. This could be good for the American deficit and economy, but sadly he will probably lack experience when it comes to domestic and foreign policies. Trump is also well known for his lack of control and rash decisions. He could be angered in a second and then the United States would be on the brink of nuclear war. Also, throughout the debates he is loud and obnoxious. Trump's real

character shines through when it comes to women and other races. Donald Trump may deny it, but he is in fact a sexist and racist. One of his foreign policy plans is to build a wall dividing the U.S. from Mexico. He says it is to increase jobs for American people, but if Americans really wanted the jobs many illegal Hispanic immigrants have, they should work harder to earn them. Trump really just wants to increase the number of whites in America and keep Hispanics out of the country. His acts of racism continue in his personal life as his company has repeatedly not rented homes to African-American families and even questioned whether President Obama was even born in America. In more recent times, Donald Trump has shown how he treats women in a voice recording that was released showing him making incredible sexist remarks about a woman who turned down his offer for sex. He also did not deny these comments on any of his social media accounts, saying it was nothing compared to what Hillary Clinton's husband has said. Trump has also been known to make other sexual remarks about women saying that all they want is a rich, powerful husband and would say that all they are is aesthetically-pleasing objects. He even would go as far as to mock Clinton on social media for her husband's past actions.

People think that not voting in an American election is wrong. They say people have fought and died for my right to vote. Our military is the greatest on earth, and I have the deepest respect for those who fight for us. They are the ones who fight to allow us to have peace in the United States. Many have died to protect our rights and freedom. Also, the fifteenth and nineteenth amendments gave African-Americans and women the right to vote in our country, which disbanded the prerogative of white men. Both groups fought for a long time to gain this right and won. So why wouldn't I vote? The key word in all of these reasons is the word "right." It may be my right to vote, but it is also my right not to vote. Since the candidates have views that I don't believe in, I am allowed to choose not to vote.

Donald Trump and Hillary Clinton are on two different sides of the political spectrum, but point in the same direction on the moral compass. The wrongdoings of both candidates have already pushed me over the edge, resulting in my choice not to vote in the 2016 election. I know that I am privileged to live in a country where I have the right to vote, since so many do not have that same liberty, but it is well known that these other countries laugh at the entertainment of American politics. I also respect all the Americans that have fought for my right to vote, though in no way am I entitled to do so. In the first Presidential election I am able to vote in, the choices I have are a liar and a racist. I choose neither.

BRITTNEY NICOLE SMITH

Though she previously attended A-State, Brittney Nicole Smith is now a Communication Media major at Bossier Parish Community College in Bossier City, Louisiana. She has plans to earn an Associates Degree with a concentration in sound and music recording because, since attending her first concert at age four, she has been fascinated with the music industry. She has now attended more than thirty concerts and hopes to one day work become a tour or artist manager for a recording label or studio.

Though music is very important to her, so are writing and traveling. She explains, "I recently traveled to Australia, New Zealand, and Fiji during the summer of 2016 after completing a trip to Ireland, London, and Wales in 2014. It was during the Australia trip that I discovered my true appreciation for life outside of the states. It is my goal to soon return to Sydney and complete a travel writing internship."

She has four pieces of advice for students writing position papers: 1) hold fast to your beliefs; 2) defend your position as though you are the central character involved in the situation, even if you're not; and 3) choose a topic that you believe in and care about so you can put your heart into the essay and mean every word you say; 4) acquire sufficient and credible research from different perspectives. While Brittney enjoys almost all types of writing genres, position papers are "by far" her favorite because, "in the midst of composing your essay, you're expressing your true inner being."

THE ASSIGNMENT: POSITION PAPER

A position paper will often require the reader to take a position on a particular topic that is currently being debated. These papers can cover anything that piques the author's interest, from local or national politics, to views on pop culture, or an issue that is currently in public discussion. When writing, the author must present a specific and clear thesis, one that takes a stand on the issue. In this assignment, there is no room for "riding the fence."

In a position paper, there is an emphasis on the use of logic to support the author's personal position. Using logos *(along with other rhetorical appeals) makes the author seem well-organized and prepared to defend his or her position instead of someone who is in the middle of a rant or tirade. Additionally, the author should validate his or her views by supporting them with researched evidence. Research in support of the author's position (or thesis) only helps strengthen the validity and intensity of the author's view in the minds of the readers. Authors should always investigate and discuss the viewpoint(s) that opposes his or her own position, as this will bring clarity and a sense of well-roundedness to the paper that allows the reader to judge the strength of the author's position in regards to the factual and practical aspects of the issue.*

Airline High School vs. ACLU

Brittney Nicole Smith

Written for Kerri Bennett's Composition I Course

· ·

For as long as print and digital press media have been in existence, religion's role in the education system has been a highly-debated topic of discussion. Many school boards, teachers, and students have been berated with allegations of inflicting religion upon their students or other members of the school. Whether the alleged events are overlooked or addressed in the courts, the issue typically comes down to the actual belief in God himself. The people of the community often spark these issues if their personal views differ from those within the school, and those with differing opinions feel that they are the ones who are being persecuted for perhaps being in the minority. This particular event happened recently at Airline High School in Bossier City, Louisiana, when the principal referenced God in online messages to the school faculty and students. Afterwards, the American Civil Liberties Union attempted to have the principal fired for this. Personally, I believe that Principal Jason Rowland and Airline High School should not suffer the potential consequences threatened by the ACLU because Rowland and the students' caring natures propelled their words and actions, not the desire to impose religion on others—the existence of the Fellowship of Christian Athletes supports this defense.

The First Amendment to the Constitution states that religious liberty is guaranteed to all Americans, along with the other freedoms of speech, expression, assembly, and press. This guarantee covers a person's right to express his or her own religious views without imposing them on the surrounding community. Specifically, principals, public school teachers, and administrators are carefully monitored for this plausible and potentially disruptive occurrence. According to the *National Coalition Against Censorship*, it must be ensured that they do not promote religion in general or promote a particular religion as being the best due to the laws of separation of church and state ("First"). These public figures are not allowed to promote prayer within the school; this is the first claim made against Jason Rowland because he included the phrase "May God Bless You All" at the end of his monthly messages (Esman). Many, especially the one who submitted the letter to the ACLU, believe that this statement was Rowland's way of forcing his students and the community to consider themselves blessed by God, and, therefore, he was trying to force them to believe in God as well. However, there is no part of Rowland's statement that supports this accusation. In fact, the use of the word "May" shows that he is merely suggesting that God bless those who are believers in his intended audience. A simpler reason proving that his statement is not breaking the law is that

Rowland is just showing love and compassion for his students, as administrators are supposed to. Rowland's long-standing spiritual involvement in church and other religious activities attributes to his continuous desire for spreading the love of God to all of whom he encounters. People of other religions who worship the same God, such as Jews and Muslims, share this same desire to wish God's blessings upon someone because it is the sincerest way to express compassion to others. This compassion extends to the students themselves with the issue of the prayer boxes in this claim. The sole existence of the prayer boxes provides a method of showing love and compassion amongst the students by praying for one another.

Student-led prayer in organizations such as FCA, which is short for Fellowship of Christian Athletes, had been declared impermissible during school-sponsored events such as football games for a long time following the case of *Santa Fe Independent School District v. Jane Doe* in 2000 because it was considered unconstitutional ("First"). Since then, prayer has been accepted at athletic events with the stipulation that administrators must not be the ones leading it; it is allowed as a student-lead activity only. Student involvement in prayer-related activities within the school is still a controversial topic, one that was addressed in the letter submitted to the ACLU which stated: "We also understand that the Fellowship of Christian Athletes has set up 'prayer boxes' with Christian symbols around Airline, with the knowledge and consent of school administrators" (Esman). Yet this claim was later discovered to be false. There was a photograph of the boxes attached to this letter stating that the installation of the boxes was to occur the following day, but that never actually happened. Nevertheless, Rowland and the members of FCA were being charged with imposing religious activities on the entire student body, despite the fact that the use of the prayer boxes would certainly not be mandatory. It would have been optional for believers, had the prayer boxes been installed. In an article published on the *Baptist Message* website, a statement was made acknowledging that the ACLU allegedly has strictly good intentions of protecting the rights and freedoms of citizens, yet in this case, they were overstepping (Blackwell). This is one of many examples of the ACLU's mission to seek and destroy all things religious.

While some believe that Airline High School is not at fault, a group of parents and other members of the ACLU and the general community would argue that Principal Rowland infringed upon the students' basic first amendment rights within the halls of his school. The letter that was written and submitted to the superintendent of the Bossier Parish School Board states that "the Constitution forbids school-sponsored prayer in order to protect those whose convictions differ from government-sanctioned beliefs" (Esman). This statement appears to support the students and protect their beliefs and best interests. However, it fails to consider the beliefs and

Airline High School vs. ACLU • Brittney Nicole Smith

Argument

interests of the students and faculty members who actually believe in God. The entire school did not participate in a large prayer event, and the prayer boxes were never distributed. Also, Rowland himself never demanded that any of his students pray throughout his time as the principal of Airline High School. Therefore, the allegation that he broke the Constitutional law is proven false. If the principal is not allowed to express compassion for his students in the sincerest way he knows how, then his fundamental rights to express himself and practice his religion are both being violated.

Members of the ACLU are confident in their stand, announcing that "Whether we're standing on principle before the highest court in the land or in state and federal courthouses across America, the ACLU wins far more often than we lose" ("ACLU History"). Interestingly enough, this is not one of those winning cases. A community prayer rally was organized and scheduled to take place surrounding the campus of Airline High School late in September following the initial complaint, one in which 1,300 people indicated their attendance (Blackwell). The community members' and students' voices were heard, and after an official hearing within the Bossier Parish School Board Meeting, it was declared that Jason Rowland was not at fault and would not suffer disciplinary actions. Although it seems to be a rare occurrence, religion won this time. Faith united the people, and love conquered, just as it should have. The effects of the ACLU's pending lawsuit against Airline High School reveal strength in numbers in the community who believes that freedom of religion should not be withheld from public school students or administrators.

Works Cited

"ACLU History." *American Civil Liberties Union.* www.aclu.org/about/aclu-history. Accessed on 16 Nov. 2016.

Blackwell, Brian. "Louisiana ACLU Accuses Airline High School, Principal of Pushing Religion—Baptist Message." *Baptist Message*, 30 Sept. 2015, baptistmessage.com/louisiana-aclu-accuses-airline-high-school-principal-of-pushing-religion/. Accessed on 16 Nov. 2016.

Esman, Marjorie. "Open Letter Regarding Official Prayer and Religious Activity at Airline High School." *Louisiana American Civil Liberties Union.* ACLU of Louisiana, 24 Sept. 2015, www.laaclu.org/press/2015/092415.htm. Accessed on 16 Nov. 2016.

"The First Amendment in Schools: Resource Guide: Religious Expression in the Public Schools." *National Coalition Against Censorship.* National Coalition Against Censorship, 01 Nov. 2016, ncac.org/resource/the-first-amendment-in-schools-resource-guide-religious-expression-in-the-public-schools. Accessed on 16 Nov. 2016.

SAMUEL VICKERS

Sam Vickers was born in Memphis, TN, but Jonesboro, AR became his hometown at the age of four when his family moved here. Upon graduating from Jonesboro High School, he enlisted in the Navy where he served for twenty years. Since his retirement, he enjoys splitting his time between working as a real estate agent and spending time with his wife and two young daughters.

Sam attributes his writing skills to his time in the Navy, believing that seeing the world and all his naval experiences helped foster his creative process. He is now a business major at Arkansas State University and is seeking his M.B.A. with a concentration in Healthcare Administration.

Sam's advice to Composition I and II students is to "open up MS Word and just start typing because too many times we are our own worst obstacle by overthinking it." He further advises his peers to "allow adequate time when writing and take frequent breaks [to get] a fresh perspective on what you have already written."

THE ASSIGNMENT: OP-ED

An "op-ed," or a piece published "opposite the editorial page," is a specific argument or view published in a magazine or newspaper, often written by an unaffiliated author independently of the paper on an issue that may or may not have been covered or confronted in the publication. Op-Eds are often confused with "editorials," opinion pieces written by the editor of the publication, and "letters to the editor," which are submitted by readers often in response to an editorial. To the contrary, op-eds are not typically written in direct response to an existing article, nor are they meant to serve as the collective opinion of the publication itself, but rather, a statement or declaration of the author's own opinionated choosing.

Op-eds typically tackle issues of relevant, modern importance. Most op-eds focus on a recent event, social turn, or public issue. The issue should be something that the author cares deeply about, and the author should have some experience or authority in the context of the issue. Op-Eds have an opinionated slant and express the author's views and feelings—whether positive, negative, or both—on the issue.

As op-eds are frequently published in public readings like magazines and newspapers, many op-eds take on a less formal tone in order to appeal to a greater variety of readers. When writing an op-ed, find an issue that is important to you, locate an expressive and well-rounded opinion about the issue, and present the opinion in an appropriately relatable way to the reader.

Argument

Cries Heard around the World

Samuel Vickers

Written for Leslie Reed's Composition I Course

· · · · · · · · · · · · · · · ·

· ·

Note: This is the rough draft of Vickers's essay, which means you may find some errors or places that need further development. It has been annotated by the instructor, Leslie Reed, to show areas that need improvement in the next draft as well as the strengths that make this essay a good example of an Op-Ed. Be sure to note the differences between the two drafts.

· ·

November 08, 2016 will be a date that goes down as one of the biggest upsets in political history that the United States has ever seen: how a multi-billionaire entrepreneur and TV reality star with no political experience became the 45th President. Since the historic night, media outlets were quick to point fingers and write elaborate stories casting blame. The major issue is that they never bothered to stop to look in the mirror. When was the last time news agencies bothered with an objective approach vise jumping on the sensationalist bandwagon of one-sided candidate bashing? Perhaps had they taken the time to report more on actual values verses focusing on rhetoric and propaganda this election result would not have come as such a surprise.

I get it, sensationalism sells and you need sales to stay in business; however, media has become a greedy, careless machine: careless because their readers are not just the American people, but the whole world. Because of their one sidedness, a clear majority of the world questions half of America right now. Wake up! Even though you might be sided with the other candidate, we are all in the same boat together. The sad fact is media is too full of itself, and cannot see the damage they are inflicting upon this great country and in turn, themselves.

I'm not sure this is the correct word here.

Can you answer this question? Sometimes, questions are best written as statements if the reader might come to a conclusion different than the point you are trying to make.

sp. and comma splice

Evaluate your thesis. What is the point you are trying to make? It appears that you have two arguments in mind: the media's bias and the media's sensationalism. Do these work together? Are they separate arguments?

Most of the essay does not speak directly to the media so you may want to reconsider the use of "you." Is this sentence directed to your audience?

The morning following the election was my own wakeup call at just how opinionated the entire world was regarding our election results. Half of my family lives in Finland and I have several friends scattered throughout the European Union, and not a one could understand how our president-elect came to be. They thought half of America had lost their mind. I viewed this as a perfect chance to understand their viewpoints and to understand a perception that went beyond our own borders. The responses I got back were eye opening, yet uniformed regardless of country. Alarmingly these answers seemed to be the same one sided rhetoric being used here by our own media outlets. This example stresses the importance of why we need our journalists to be true to their calling. You are not just informing American citizens, but the entire world is listening and watching.

Now amidst all the upset there are a few news personalities that are starting to get it. The morning following the election results, Joe Scarborough with MSNBC took some ownership as well as faulting other media outlets saying that months prior many news personalities had formed opinions on the election outcome which influenced their writing. Scarborough even claimed that during this time had any journalists even suggested the possibility of the other candidate winning, their journalistic standards came into question. So not only do we have a one-sided story, but now those media outlets with the responsibility to report the news objectively have virtually become a bully to any journalist just trying to do their job correctly and report the other side of the story.

Good job showing more than one viewpoint!

Could you add source material to substantiate the claim of bias?

In light of Scarborough's election reflection, mainstream media is not entirely at fault with misinforming readers. As social media grows, more people are connected than ever before and that allows room for fake news altogether. Jim Rutenberg with the New York Times wrote a piece "Media's Next Challenge: Overcoming the Threat of Fake News." His article explains the struggle of mainstream media, selling papers and its battle with the increasing popularity of social media news outlets. He goes on to say that papers are not selling as much; therefore, their answer is to cut staff and departments which brings us to a scary "catch 22." Rutenberg warns, "It means another rapid depletion in the nation's ranks of traditionally trained journalists whose main mission is to root out corruption, hold the powerful accountable and sort fact from fiction for voters." So, in recap, as social media increases in popularity, papers lose sales which directly results in laid off journalist. Now our unemployed journalists are seeking jobs with social media news outlets and in turn can lower their journalistic standards. Thus, bringing us back to papers losing more sales.

In closing, the saddest part of this election was not who won and who lost, but the sheer shock and surprise so many experienced at the outcome. In their minds, this was going to be a shutout victory. How did so many Americans get it wrong? Because they were not properly informed. Why were they not properly informed? Because journalistic standards fell drastically, were written from opinions vise objectivity or were false to begin with. What's worse is that our media outlets have not even begun to feel the repercussion for such one-sidedness. Half of America already questioned their integrity and now the other half, the losing half will look back and begin to question their creditability as well. The collateral damage will be a loss in sales causing that catch 22 amongst journalists that Jim Rutenberg wrote about. Finally, the biggest revelation of all, sure sensationalism sells but it will not be long lasting if the public does not perceive you as a true objective journalist which did not occur during the 2016 election.

This conclusion has a nice sentiment and reinforces that this is about the media and not necessarily politics.

This sentence is unclear. Do you mean to say that "articles were written from opinions instead of objectivity?"

Not only have you provided an exigency for your current argument, but you've paved the way for a follow-up project! Good work!

sp.

Works Cited

Scarborough, Joe. "Morning Joe." MSNBC, commentary by Joe Scarborough and Mika Brzezinski, 10 Nov. 2016.

Rutenberg, Jim. "Media's Next Challenge: Overcoming the Threat of Fake News." The New York Times, 6 Nov. 2016, https://www.nytimes.com/2016/11/07/business/media/medias-next-challenge-overcoming-the-threat-of-fake-news.html.

See MLA format. Citations should be in alphabetical order, hanging indents should be used, and the "http://" should be omitted from the citation. Also, remember to use italics for the titles of longer works like newspapers.

Cries Heard around the World

Samuel Vickers

Written for Leslie Reed's Composition I Course

Note: This is the polished draft of Vickers's essay. It has been revised by the author after receiving feedback from the instructor.

November 08, 2016 will be a date that goes down as one of the biggest upsets in political history that the United States has ever seen: how a multi-billionaire entrepreneur and TV reality star with no political experience became the 45th President. Since the historic night, news media from all sources were amazed at the upset and dumbfounded as to just how this happened. Major networks, newspapers and social media have been quick to write about their opinions on the matter but I am here to share the secret and the answer is simple. Journalism 101.

So, what is journalism 101? It is thorough research on the whole story, which means an equal, unbiased focus on both political parties. In the months leading up to the election, most media outlets became very one-sided and eventually this election turned into a sensationalist bandwagon of one-sided candidate bashing. Perhaps had they remained neutral and not allowed the tone of their reporting to come across as rhetoric and propaganda, then perhaps the media's tone the following morning would not have been one of surprise and wonderment as to how this upset occurred.

I get it; sensationalism sells and all media outlets need sales to stay in business. However, it has become a greedy, careless machine: careless because their readers are not just the American people, but the whole world. Because of their one sidedness, numerous countries throughout the world questions half of America right now. Wake up! Even though you might be sided with the other candidate, we are all in the same boat together. The sad fact is media is too full of itself and cannot see the damage they are inflicting upon this great country and in turn, themselves.

The morning following the election was my own wakeup call, which stressed the importance for our media outlets to get back to basics and give equal, unbiased news. I say it was my own wakeup call because I saw just how opinionated parts of the world was regarding our election results. My in-laws live in Finland, and through my military career, I had the wonderful opportunity to have several friendships scattered throughout the European

Union. The morning after election night, neither my in-laws nor my friends could understand how our president-elect came to be. They thought half of America had lost their minds. I viewed this as a perfect chance to understand their viewpoints and to understand a perception that went beyond our own country.

What I discovered is that friends and family alike, regardless of country had an alarming one sided view of this election which mirrored the same surprise and wonderment that our media had the following morning. The younger the generation, the more likely they were to obtain their news from just social media. The older generation, especially my in-laws, would read about various U.S. election topics from their local paper or news station. Their articles in the paper and the news segments were taken from our own national agencies and just repackaged for local translations. This example stresses the importance of why we need our journalists to be true to their calling. They are not just informing American citizens; the entire world is listening and watching.

Now amidst all the upset, there are a few news personalities that are starting to own up towards not practicing Journalism 101. The morning following the election results, Joe Scarborough with MSNBC took some ownership as well as faulting other media outlets saying that months prior many news personalities had formed opinions on the election outcome which influenced their writing. Scarborough even claimed that during this time had any journalists even suggested the possibility of the other candidate winning, their journalistic standards came into question. So not only do we have a one-sided story, but now those media outlets with the responsibility to report the news objectively have virtually become a bully to any journalist just trying to do their job correctly and report the other side of the story.

In light of Scarborough's election reflection, I am a firm believer in karma and right now the media is beginning to feel the effects of being biased during this election. In one poll, over 78 percent felt that the media coverage of the 2016 presidential campaign was biased. Regardless of which political party you affiliate with, America as a whole is sick of the news and is starting to turn away to avoid it all together. Jennifer Harper of *The Washington Times* wrote an article about how media is paying the price for their biased writings in "Price of bias: America now shunning news media after 2016 election." The article shows that statically, America is fed up and that very little news puts them in a good mood, therefore why watch or read it.

Now mainstream media is not entirely at fault with misinforming readers. Unfortunately, as social media grows, it allows anyone to create a story and I say story because that is exactly what you might be getting.

Social media does not have to follow a certain standard and it certainly does not have to follow journalistic standards. Social media is becoming more and more popular; therefore, we need to be very vigilant about separating fact from fiction. As a matter of fact, social media and fake news was a main article in the *New York Times* just last week.

Jim Rutenberg with the *New York Times* wrote a piece "Media's Next Challenge: Overcoming the Threat of Fake News." His article explains the struggle of mainstream media, selling papers and its battle with the increasing popularity of social media news outlets. He goes on to say that papers are not selling as much; therefore, their answer is to cut staff and departments which brings us to a scary "catch 22." Rutenberg further warns, "It means another rapid depletion in the nation's ranks of traditionally trained journalists whose main mission is to root out corruption, hold the powerful accountable and sort fact from fiction for voters." So, in short, as social media increases in popularity, papers lose sales, which directly results in laid off journalists. Now our unemployed journalists are seeking jobs with social media news outlets and in turn can lower their journalistic standards. Thus, bringing us back to papers losing more sales.

In closing, the saddest part of this election was not who won and who lost, but the sheer fact that so many media outlets lowered their standards or had none at all. One issue that should concern our media is that they might not have even begun to feel the repercussion for such one-sidedness. Half of America already questioned their integrity and now the other half, the losing half might look back and begin to question their credibility as well. The potential collateral damage would be that loss in sales causing that "catch 22" amongst journalists that Jim Rutenberg wrote about. Finally, the biggest revelation of all, sure sensationalism sells, but it will not be long lasting if the public does not perceive you as a true objective journalist which did not occur during the 2016 election.

Works Cited

Harper, Jennifer. "Price of Bias: America Now Shunning News Media after 2016 Election." *The Washington Times*, 15 Nov. 2016, www.washingtontimes.com/news/2016/nov/15/america-avoiding-the-news-media-after-2016-electio/.

Rutenberg, Jim. "Media's Next Challenge: Overcoming the Threat of Fake News." *The New York Times*, 6 Nov. 2016, www.nytimes.com/2016/11/07/business/media/medias-next-challenge-overcoming-the-threat-of-fake-news.html.

Scarborough, Joe, host. *Morning Joe*. MSNBC, 10 Nov. 2016.

Student Style Manual

Citing in the Disciplines

Kristi Costello

Assistant Professor of Composition, Rhetoric, and Writing Studies at Arkansas State University

· ·

WHEN AND WHY WE CITE

You have likely heard a collective groan anytime the professor at the front of the room explains that the paper she's just assigned needs to be in a specific style, such as APA (American Psychological Association), AP (Associated Press), CMS (Chicago Manual of Style), MLA (Modern Language Association), or Turabian, but universities require students to cite sources for several reasons:

• To give credit to others for their ideas;

• To provide information to readers so they can find the sources themselves;

• To lend credibility to the author's claims;

• To distance themselves from someone else's ideas.

While it is a good practice to give credit to anyone whose words or ideas you share, it is especially important in institutions of higher learning because faculty and students are held accountable for their work. In higher education, one's writing and research can help him or her obtain publication, tenure, grants, and prestige. However, more importantly, when shared with others, one's ideas, writing, methods, and research can lead to new and improved ideas, writing, methods, and research. This process of sharing and building on one another's ideas has led to life-changing scientific advancements, new perspectives on canonical texts, policy reforms, and social and political movements. In Kenneth Burke's *The Philosophy of Literary Form*, he describes this process as an ongoing conversation. He writes:

> Imagine that you enter a parlor. You come late. When you arrive, others have long preceded you, and they are engaged in a heated discussion, a discussion too heated for them to pause and tell you exactly what it is about. In fact, the discussion had already begun long before any of them got there, so that no one present is qualified to retrace for you all the steps that had gone before. You listen for a while, until you decide that you have caught the tenor of the argument; then you put in your oar. Someone answers; you answer him; another comes to your defense; another aligns himself against you, to either the embarrassment or gratification of your opponent, depending upon the quality

Citing in the Disciplines

of your ally's assistance. However, the discussion is interminable. The hour grows late, you must depart. And you do depart, with the discussion still vigorously in progress. (110–111)

Thus, if you think about knowledge and the generation of knowledge as unending conversation, it becomes clear that everyone who had a voice in the conversation deserves to be heard and know he or she was heard. Even when we're refuting their ideas, research, or methods,.they still deserve credit for being a part of the conversation because it may have been their finding or mistake that led to the next improvement or advancement. It is also equally important to interrogate the conversation, asking yourself whose voices have been left out and why.

In sum, any time you bring someone else's ideas or work into your writing, you should cite the source. The only time you need not cite is when the information is common knowledge. For example, you would not need to cite that Thomas Jefferson was the third president of the United States of America, but you would want to cite that President Jefferson gave of more than 6,000 of his own books to replenish the Library of Congress after arson perpetrated by British soldiers depleted the library's holdings ("10 things you didn't know about Thomas Jefferson"). When in doubt as to whether information should be cited, cite it. It is always better to over-cite than under-cite. To see essays formatted according to each style guide, please see the examples provided for you in the "Sample Papers in MLA, Chicago, and APA Styles" section.

• •

WRITE about an instance in which someone was accused of plagiarism. It can be your own experience or that of a friend, politician, or celebrity. What do you recall about the story? Was it plagiarism? How did people react? What impact did the allegation have on the accused?

• •

Works Cited

"10 things you didn't know about Thomas Jefferson." *The Washington Post*, 30 June 2011, www.washingtonpost.com/lifestyle/kidspost/10-things-you-didnt-know-about-thomas-jefferson/2011/04/12/AGGLlWsH_story.html?utm_term=.03d87ec3f8a9#comments. Accessed 6 Feb. 2017.

Burke, Kenneth. *The Philosophy of Literary Form*. University of California Press, 1941.

Shit Academics Say
5 hrs · 🌐

To err is human. To err repeatedly is research.

Student Style Manual for MLA, Chicago, and APA Documentation

MLA Style

The Modern Language Association of America, or MLA, developed a style guide to establish rules and bring consistency to written academic works. The *MLA Handbook* is most often used in the language arts and humanities disciplines, including literature, literary criticism, English studies, and cultural studies. The most recent publication, the 8th edition, was published in 2016.

MLA Guidelines for Formatting Papers

An MLA essay follows formatting guidelines:

- The essay should be typed, double spaced in 12-point font size without additional spacing between paragraphs, in an easy-to-read font (such as Times New Roman) on 8.5-inch by 11-inch paper, with 1-inch margins on all sides.

- Do not include a title page unless required to do so. The first page of the essay should include the author's name, instructor's name, course information, and the date the essay is due. This information should be double spaced and placed in the upper left corner of the page, beginning one inch from the top.

- The title should follow the author and course information and should be centered, in title case (uppercase and lowercase letters), with no underlining, italicizing, or bolding.

- Starting on the first page, each page should have a running header in the right corner, 1/2 inch from the top margin and flush with the right margin, which includes the author's last name and the page number.

- Use the tab key or your ruler to indent the first line of each paragraph 1/2 inch from the left margin.

- Use only one space after periods or other punctuation marks.

- Commas and periods go inside the quotation marks, not outside: "Chapter 1," rather than "Chapter 1", for example.

- Use em dashes (—) and ellipses (...) and replace hyphens (-) with en dashes (–) where appropriate, and make consistent.

MLA General In-Text Citation Rules

MLA Style

Including source information in parentheses after a quote or paraphrase is known as parenthetical citation, and is required when using MLA style.

In MLA, it is important to provide a lead-in or introductory phrase for source quotations, paraphrases, or summaries in the text, especially the first time the source is used. Lead-ins introduce the sources to the audience and provide a smooth transition from the student author's writing to quotes, summaries, and paraphrases within the text. When the author's name is mentioned in the signal phrase, you do not need to include it in the in-text citation, rather use the page number alone, if the source is paginated. However, you will need to continue to include the author's last name in subsequent uses.

Example: Introducing Sources with a Lead-In

As Glenn and Ratcliffe explain in *Silence and Listening as Rhetorical Arts*, we "can more productively discern and implement actions that are more ethical, efficient, and appropriate when all parties agree to engage in rhetorical situations that include not only respectful speaking, reading, and writing, but also productive silence and rhetorical listening" (3).

In-Text Citations: Print Sources

A Work by a Single Author
The author's last name and the page numbers (when available) from the source material should appear in the text. The relevant page numbers appear in the parenthetical citation, not in the text.

Examples
Shor argues that basic writing is "a containment track below freshman comp, a gate below the gate" (94).

Basic writing is "a containment track below freshman comp, a gate below the gate" (Shor 94).

Block Quotations

Begin quotations more than four lines in length on a new line that is indented one inch from the left margin. Place the whole quote, double spaced, within the new margin. Do not use quotation marks. Note that the parenthetical citation comes after the end punctuation.

As a builder, Lubbers was tasked to determine the most effective method for ensuring the safety and integrity of structures in a variety of climates. Lubbers's study found the following:

> The prevailing wind being forecast for January 2 will be from the southwest, and will reach speeds of up to 50 miles per hour. This wind has the potential to cause significant damage to the current construction. The building should be braced heavily to avoid collapse. (202)

Unknown Author

When the author is not known, use an abbreviated title of the source in the parenthetical citation. Use quotation marks for titles of short works (articles, chapters, episodes, songs) and italics for titles of longer works (movies, books, television shows), and include a page number.

The results of the study on multitasking showed that switching from one task to another actually takes more time than giving attention to one task at a time ("Is Multitasking More Efficient?" 6).

Authors with Same Last Name

If two or more cited authors have the same last name, include both authors' first initials. If different authors share the same first initial, provide the authors' full names.

Although some researchers have found that multitasking is actually counterproductive and inefficient (K. Jones 12), more and more students are employing multitasking in their daily lives (P. Jones 46).

Two Works by the Same Author

To cite two or more sources by the same author, include the title (or abbreviated title) in the parentheses, preceding the page number.

Bartholomae states that to be successful, college students must invent a language they feel places them in the realm of academia ("Inventing the University" 146), and argues that basic writing programs both preserve and attempt to bridge cultural differences in the classroom ("The Tidy House" 87).

MLA Style

A Work by Two or Three Authors
If a source has two or three authors, provide the authors' last names in the text or in parentheses.

Collins and Blum outline the way socioeconomics and politics outside the university also play a role in instigating the division between "basic" and "normal" writers (14).

The authors outline the way socioeconomics and politics outside the university also play a role in instigating the division between "basic" and "normal" writers (Collins and Blum 14).

A Work by More than Three Authors
For more than three authors, include the first author's last name followed by et al., or give the last name of each author.

Cincotta et al. assert that the launch of Sputnik expanded the competitive arena between the U.S. and the Soviet Union (68).

Historians assert that the launch of Sputnik expanded the competitive arena between the U.S. and the Soviet Union (Cincotta et al. 68).

Cincotta, Brown, Burant, Green, Holden, and Marshall assert that the launch of Sputnik expanded the competitive arena between the U.S. and the Soviet Union (68).

Indirect Sources
It may sometimes be necessary to use a work that has been cited in another source. For such indirect or secondary sources, use "qtd. in" to indicate the primary source.

According to Harvey Graff, "We do not know what we mean by literacy" (qtd. in Lunsford 252).

Encyclopedia/Dictionary Entry
Use the term being cited in quotation marks for the parenthetical citation of this type of source.

A citation is a "quotation from or reference to a book, paper, or author" ("Citation").

Electronic Sources

For electronic sources, include the first item (author name, title, etc.) in the Works Cited entry that corresponds to the citation.

Do not include URLs in the text unless absolutely necessary; if included, make the URL as brief as possible, such as npr.org rather than http://www.npr.org.

Web Site

A similar study determined that subjects lost more time when switching from a familiar task to an unfamiliar task ("Is Multitasking").

Film

Big Fish, directed by Tim Burton, details the extraordinary life of Edward Bloom (2003).

Television

In *Criminal Minds*, a suspect awakens from a coma with no memory of having committed the crimes he is accused of ("Tabula Rasa").

MLA WORKS CITED PAGE

A Works Cited must be included at the end of the paper. Each source cited in the text must have a corresponding Works Cited entry.

- Begin the Works Cited on a separate page, formatted with one-inch margins and running header that contains a last name and page number, which continues from the last page of the essay. Center the words Works Cited as the title at the top of the page. Do not use italics, bolding, underlining, or quotation marks.

- List entries alphabetically by the author's (or editor's) last name, using last name, first name format. Do not list titles (e.g., Dr.) or degrees (e.g., PhD), but include suffixes such as "Jr." (e.g., Gates, Henry Louis, Jr.).

- Use a hanging indent for each entry more than one line in length. Double space all citations, and do not add extra spaces between entries.

- Capitalize each word in the title, with the exception of conjunctions, prepositions, or articles (such as a, an, the) unless it is the first word of the title or subtitle: *Everything Is Illuminated*, *The Art of War*, *For Whom the Bell Tolls*.

- List page numbers efficiently. For example, if referencing a work that appeared on pages 136 through 153, list the page numbers as 136–53.

- Use italics for larger works (books, movies, magazines) and quotation marks for shorter works (articles, songs, essays, poems).

MLA 8: The Works Cited List

Given that new mediums are being introduced constantly and some publication types now include more than one medium or blur the lines between traditional mediums, MLA 8 included a general list to follow for citing sources to ensure that any source can be cited in MLA—even those that have not yet been created. Note that the punctuation that follows each element is the punctuation that should be included in your Works Cited, though your Works Cited entry will always end with a period.

1. Author.
2. Title of Source.
3. Title of Container,
4. Other Contributors,
5. Version,
6. Number,
7. Publisher,
8. Publication date,
9. Page number/s preceded by p. or pp.,
10. Location (If important).

Example 1: Citing the Full Book

Allen, Jason. *A Meditation on Fire: Poems.* Southeast Missouri State University Press, 2016.

Example 2: Citing Part of the Book

Allen, Jason. "Uncle Jeff Jumped Out a Window." *A Meditation on Fire: Poems,* Southeast Missouri State University Press, 2016, p. 25.

Rodrigueź, Jose Antonio. "The Little Rooms." *The Shallow End of Sleep,* Tiá Chucha Press, 2011, pp. 76–77.

Note that because Allen's poem, "Uncle Jeff Jumped Out a Window" is only one page, we use "p. 25" in the Works Cited entry. Since Rodriguez's poem is two pages, we use "pp. 76–77."

MLA 8 uses the term "container" to indicate the site of a given source, such as the website that houses the article or the journal from which an article came. If a source has multiple containers (e.g., the article came from a journal found in ProQuest), your citation may extend beyond the directions above. Consult the chart below for assistance with sources with more than one container.

1   Author.
2. Title.
3. Title of container,
4. Other contributors (translators or editors),

5. Version (edition),
6. Number (vol. and/or no.),
7. Publisher,
8. Publisher Date,
9. Location,
10. Page Numbers (preceded with p. or pp.).
11. 2nd container's title,
12. Other contributors,
13. Version,
14. Number,
15. Publisher,
16. Date of Publication,
17. Location (if necessary).

Print Sources

Books

One Author
When a book has one author, list the author's name in last name, first name format.

Sedaris, David. *Barrel Fever*. Little, Brown, 1994.

Two or Three Authors
Use the last name, first name format for the first author; then list other author names by first name, last name.

Ward, Geoffrey, Ken Burns, and Kevin Baker. *Baseball: An Illustrated History*. Alfred A. Knopf, Inc., 1996.

Three or More Authors
For more than three authors, you may include each author's name, or you may list only the first author followed by et al., rather than listing the additional authors' names. The et in et al. should not be followed by a period.

Barnes, Sonya, et al. *Image Power: Top Image Experts Share What to Know to Look Your Best*. PowerDynamics Publishing, 2008.

Two or More Works by the Same Author
For more than one work by the same author, list the entries alphabetically by title, and use three hyphens rather than the author's name for each entry after the first:

Bartholomae, David. "Inventing the University." [...]

---. "The Tidy House: Basic Writing in the American Curriculum." [...]

MLA Style

Work by an Unknown Author
Works by an unknown author should be alphabetized by their title.

Beowulf. [...]

Author with an Editor
Begin with the author, then include the editor after the title.

Fielding, Henry. *Tom Jones.* Edited by Sheridan Baker, W. W. Norton & Company, Inc., 1973.

Editor with no Author
Begin with the title of the piece, then provide the editor name.

Che: The Life, Death, and Afterlife of a Revolutionary. Edited by Joseph Hart, Thunder's Mouth Press, 2003.

Author with a Translator
List the entry by author name, then include the translator after the title.

Gide, André. *Lafcadio's Adventures.* Translated by Dorothy Bussy, Vintage Books, 1953.

A Work in an Anthology
Begin with the author name, then the title of the article or chapter in quotation marks. List the anthology title in italics, followed by the editor's name.

Bartholomae, David. "Inventing the University." *When a Writer Can't Write.* Edited by Mike Rose, Guilford, 1985, pp. 134–65.

Encyclopedia/Dictionary Entry
For entries in reference works, cite the entry by the term being referenced. Do not include publisher information or page number.

"Citation." *The Shorter Oxford English Dictionary.* 5th ed., 2002.

Periodicals
List the author of the article first, then include the article title in quotation marks and the periodical title in italics. Follow with the date of publication, and abbreviate all months.

Article in a Magazine
Miller, Jeremy. "The Tyranny of the Test: One Year as a Kaplan Coach in the Public Schools." *Harper's Magazine,* 2 Sept. 2008, pp. 35–46.

Article in a Newspaper
Timson, Judith. "Stop All That Multitasking, Study Suggests." *The Toronto Star,* 7 Aug. 2001, p. E2.

Article in a Scholarly Journal
Provide issue numbers, when available.

Collins, Terence, and Melissa Blum. "Meanness and Failure: Sanctioning Basic Writers." *Journal of Basic Writing*, vol. 19, no. 1, 2000, pp. 13–21.

Personal Interview/Personal Communication
Personal interviews are interviews you conduct yourself. List the interview by the name of the interviewee and include "Personal interview" and the date of the interview.

Smith, Jane. Personal interview. 19 May 2014.

Electronic Sources
Because web sites are often updated and the same information may not be available later, it is a good practice to list your date of access, even though MLA 8 does not require it.

Web Site
List the name of the organization hosting the web site, followed by the name of the site. Use n.d. if no publishing date is given. Include the DOI or Permalink if available, otherwise include the URL (without http://), followed by the date of access.

National Public Radio. *Morning Edition*. NPR, 14 Jan. 2014, www.npr.org/ programs/morning-edition. Accessed 26 Apr. 2014.

Web Page
List the author if known, followed by the information required for web sites.

Abdullah, Mardziah Hayati. "The Impact of Electronic Communication on Writing." *EricDigests.org*. ERIC Clearinghouse on Reading, English, and Communication, Dec. 2003, www.ericdigests.org/2004-1/impact.htm. Accessed 13 Oct. 2004.

Online Book
List the entry by author name, title of book in italics, followed by the organization hosting the page.

Austen, Jane. *Pride and Prejudice*. Project Gutenberg, 2013, www.gutenberg. org/files/1342/1342-h/1342-h.htm. Accessed 14 Apr. 2014.

Article in an Online Magazine
Start with the author name, followed by the article name in quotation marks, title of the online magazine in italics, publisher name, publication date, medium, and date of access.

Remnick, David. "Putin and the Exile." *New Yorker*. NewYorker.com, 28 Apr. 2014, www.newyorker.com/magazine/2014/04/28/putin-and-the-exile. Accessed 28 Apr. 2014.

MLA Style

Article in an Online Scholarly Journal

Use the same format as a scholarly journal in print, but include the DOI or permalink and list the date of access.

Soliday, Mary. "From the Margins to the Mainstream: Reconceiving Remediation." *College Composition and Communication*, vol. 47, no. 1, 1996, pp. 85–100, www.jstor.org/stable/358275. Accessed 14 Jan. 2014.

Film

List films by their title in italics, followed by the director's name, then list performer names if relevant. Follow with the distributor and release year.

The Wolf of Wall Street. Directed by Martin Scorsese, performances by Leonardo DiCaprio, Jonah Hill, Matthew McConaughey, Kyle Chandler, and Jon Favreau, Paramount, 2013.

Broadcast Program

Begin with the title of the episode in quotation marks, then the name of the program in italics. Include the network name, call letters of the station and the city, and broadcast date.

"Unsolvable." *Brooklyn Nine-Nine*. Fox, WXMI, Grand Rapids, 19 Mar. 2014.

Recorded Episode

List the entry by episode name in quotation marks, followed by the series name in italics, the distributor name, and the date of distribution.

"Tabula Rasa." *Criminal Minds: Season 3*, written by Jeff Davis, Dan Sworkin, and Jay Beattie, directed by Steve Boyum, Paramount, 2010.

Music or Sound Recording

Begin with the artist name, then put song titles in quotation marks and album names in italics. If relevant, list composer or performer information after the album title. Include the recording company and publication date (or n.d., if date is unknown).

The Beatles. *Revolver*. EMI, 2009.

Beyoncé. "Pray You Catch Me." *Lemonade*, Parkwood Entertainment, 2016, www.beyonce.com/album/lemonade-visual-album/. Accessed 6 Feb. 2017.

Miranda, Lin-Manuel. *The Hamilton Mixtape*, Atlantic Records, 2016.

Yo-Yo Ma. *Yo-Yo Ma Plays Ennio Morricone*, composed by Ennio Morricone, Sony Masterworks, 2010.

Chicago Style (CMS)

The *Chicago Manual of Style*, or CMS, is a style guide created by the University of Chicago Press in the early twentieth century, to establish formatting rules and bring consistency to their publications. Chicago style is most often used in the social sciences, arts, and humanities disciplines, such as history, art, philosophy, music, theatre, and religious studies. The most recent publication, the 16th edition, was published in 2010.

CMS GUIDELINES FOR FORMATTING PAPERS

- The essay should be typed, double spaced in 12-point font size, in an easy-to-read font (such as Times New Roman) on 8.5-inch by 11-inch paper, with 1-inch margins on all sides.

- Include a title page, with the title centered a third of the way down the page, and the author's name and any other relevant information centered a few lines down from the title.

- Paginate the essay in the top right corner of the page, beginning with the first page of the text (not the title page).

- Change underlining to italics. However, some underlining may need to be preserved, depending on the original material.

- Fix commas and periods relative to quotation marks (commas and periods go inside the quotation marks, not outside: "Chapter 1," rather than "Chapter 1", for example).

- Use em dashes (—) and ellipses (…) where appropriate, and make consistent.

- Replace hyphens (-) with en dashes (–) where appropriate.

- Leave one character space, rather than two spaces, between words and sentences and after colons.

- Use double spacing for text, except in block quotations. Use single spacing for footnotes and bibliography/reference lists, with a line to separate entries.

- The bibliography should begin on a new page, separate from the essay.

CMS GENERAL IN-TEXT CITATION AND FOOTNOTE RULES

CMS In-Text Citations and Footnotes

Note Numbers

Note reference numbers in text are superscripted. In the notes themselves, they are full size and followed by a period.

Sedaris recalls, "We rode round and round the block on our pony, who groaned beneath the collective weight of our rich and overwhelming capacity for love and understanding."[1]

> 1. David Sedaris, *Barrel Fever* (New York: Little, Brown, 1994), 9–10.

Notes should be numbered consecutively, beginning with 1, throughout the essay. A note number should generally be placed at the end of a sentence, a clause, or a quotation. The number follows any punctuation mark except for the dash, which it precedes.

Many students argue that they work better when multitasking[5]—but research suggests this may not be the case.

Bibliographic citations are provided in footnotes (which appear at the bottom of a page), supplemented by a bibliography at the end of the work. Footnotes are numbered (but not superscripted) and correspond to superscripted note reference numbers in the text.

Full Footnote Citation

> 1. David Sedaris, *Barrel Fever* (New York: Little, Brown, 1994), 36–37.

Short Footnote Citation

> 1. Sedaris, *Barrel Fever*, 36–37.

Entry in a Bibliography

> Sedaris, David. *Barrel Fever*. New York: Little, Brown. 1994.

If the same source is used consecutively in the text, the source should be formatted as usual for the first entry, and "Ibid." and the relevant page number, if different than the first note, should be used for each subsequent entry, until a different source is used within the text.

> 1. David Sedaris, *Barrel Fever* (New York: Little, Brown, 1994), 36.

> 2. Ibid.

> 3. Ibid., 37.

> 4. David Bartholomae, "Inventing the University," in *When a Writer Can't Write*, ed. Mike Rose (New York: Guilford, 1985), 146.

Shortened Citations

Because the complete citation information is available in the corresponding bibliography, using the short footnote citation is acceptable in Chicago style.

The short form of a citation should include enough information to lead readers to the appropriate entry in the bibliography. The short form consists of the last name of the author, the main title of the work cited (usually shortened if more than four words), and the page number indicating where the information is located.

1. David Bartholomae, "Inventing the University," in *When a Writer Can't Write*, ed. Mike Rose (New York: Guilford, 1985), 146.

2. Bartholomae, "Inventing the University," 146.

Using In-Text Sources

It is important to provide a lead-in to source quotations, summaries, or paraphrases in the text, especially the first time the source is used. Lead-ins introduce the sources to the audience and provide a smooth transition from the author's writing to quotes, summaries, and paraphrases within the text.

Block Quotations

For quotations longer than four lines in length, add an extra line space and indent 1/2 inch from the left margin. Place the whole quote, single spaced, within the new margin. Do not use quotation marks. The note number should come after the end punctuation.

As a builder, Lubbers was tasked to determine the most effective method for ensuring the safety and integrity of structures in a variety of climates. Lubbers's study found the following:

> The prevailing wind being forecast for January 2 will be from the southwest, and will reach speeds of up to 50 miles per hour. This wind has the potential to cause significant damage to the current construction. The building should be braced heavily to avoid collapse.[3]

Because the formatting for footnotes is consistent regardless of the medium being cited, not all areas that follow will include in-text citation examples.

Books

One Author

In-Text Citation

Sedaris recalls, "We rode round and round the block on our pony, who groaned beneath the collective weight of our rich and overwhelming capacity for love and understanding."[1]

Short Footnote Citation

1. Sedaris, *Barrel Fever*, 9–10.

Two to Three Authors

In-Text Citation

Collins and Blum outline the way socioeconomics and politics outside the university also play a role in instigating the division between "basic" and "normal" writers.[3]

Short Footnote Citation

> 3. Collins and Blum, "Meanness and Failure," 14.

More than Three Authors

In-Text Citation

Cincotta et al. assert that the launch of Sputnik expanded the competitive arena between the U.S. and the Soviet Union.[2]

Short Footnote Citation

> 2. Howard Cincotta et al., *An Outline of American History* (Washington D.C.: United States Information Agency, 1994).

Unknown Author

In-Text Citation

A study determined that subjects lose time when switching from task to task.[4]

Short Footnote Citation

> 4. "Is Multitasking," 3.

Editor as Author

This type of source includes information written by the editor of an anthology, as in a foreword, introduction, afterword, or editor's notes. In these cases, the editor should be treated as the author of the source being used.

In-Text Citation

Historian Joseph Hart asserts, "Ernesto Che Guevara's death at the hands of Bolivian troops last October enhanced a legend that began when he was Fidel Castro's right-hand man in Cuba."[5]

Short Footnote Citation

> 5. Hart, *Che*, 3.

Bibliography Entry

Hart, Joseph, ed. *Che: The Life, Death, and Afterlife of a Revolutionary*. New York: Thunder's Mouth Press, 2003.

Work in an Anthology

Please note that in these cases, the author of the work being quoted will be the primary reference in the text, the footnote, and the bibliography; the anthology editor(s) will also be included in the bibliography entry. A bibliography entry is included here as an example.

In-Text Citation

According to David Bartholomae, students who were less successful at this "invention" were considered basic writers; those who were more successful were not.[6]

Long Footnote Citation

6. David Bartholomae, "Inventing the University," in *When a Writer Can't Write*, ed. Mike Rose (New York: Guilford, 1985), 134–65.

Short Footnote Citation

6. Bartholomae, "Inventing the University," 146–47.

Bibliography Entry

Bartholomae, David. "Inventing the University." In *When a Writer Can't Write*, edited by Mike Rose, 134–65. New York: Guilford, 1985.

Periodicals

Article in a Journal

In-Text Citation

Teacher-researchers Terence Collins and Melissa Blum pointed to the ways that socioeconomics and politics outside of the university also played a role in instigating the division between "basic" and "normal" writers.[7]

Short Footnote Citation

7. Collins and Blum, "Meanness and Failure," 14.

Article in a Magazine

Short Footnote Citation

8. Miller, "The Tyranny of the Test," 39.

Article in a Newspaper

Note that Chicago style does not require newspaper articles to be included in the bibliography, as long as they have been included in the text and footnotes. In these cases, however, the long footnote citation should be used.

Long Footnote Citation

9. Eric Pianin, "Use of Arsenic in Wood Products to End," *Washington Post*, February 13, 2002, final edition.

Entry in an Encyclopedia/Dictionary

Though cited in the footnotes, well-known reference materials are typically not cited in the bibiliography, and the publication information is often omitted. If the publication is not the first edition, the edition number must be included.

Footnote Citation

10. *The Shorter Oxford English Dictionary*, 5th ed., s.v. "citation."

Personal Interview/Personal Communication

Personal interviews are included as a note only; they do not need to be included in the bibliography.

11. Danny Williams, e-mail message to author, June 15, 2017.

Electronic Sources

Article from an Online Periodical

Follow the same guidelines as printed articles and include the URL or, if available, the digital object identifier (DOI).

Scholarly Journal

12. Adler-Kassner and Harrington, "Responsibility and Composition's Future," 77. http://www.jstor.org/discover/10.2307/27917885?uid=3739728 &uid=2129&uid=2&uid=70&uid=4&uid=3739256&sid=21104117601803.

Article in a Popular Magazine

13. Remnick, "Putin and the Exile." http://www.newyorker.com/talk/comment/2014/04/28/140428taco_talk_remnick.

Online Newspaper Article

Remember that Chicago style does not require newspaper articles to be included in the bibiliography. Additionally, a URL need not be included for online newspaper sources; however, the long footnote citation must be used.

Long Footnote Citation

14. Felicia R. Lee, "Trying to Bring Baldwin's Complex Voice Back," *The New York Times*, April 24, 2014.

Online Encyclopedia/Dictionary Entry

15. *Merriam-Webster Online*, s.v. "citation," accessed April 26, 2014, http://www.merriam-webster.com/dictionary/citation.

Film

16. *Big Fish*, directed by Tim Burton. (2003; Culver City, CA: Sony Home Pictures Entertainment, 2004), DVD.

Single Episode of a Television Series

17. Jeff Davis, Dan Sworkin, and Jay Beattie, "Tabula Rasa." *Criminal Minds,* season 3, episode 19, directed by Steve Boyum, aired May 14, 2008. (Los Angeles, CA: Paramount, 2010), DVD.

Music or Sound Recording

Album

18. The Beatles, *Revolver*, EMI, 2009, CD.

Song

19. Miranda Lambert, vocal performance of "Heart Like Mine," by Travis Howard, Miranda Lambert, and Ashley Monroe, recorded 2009, on *Revolution*, Columbia Nashville, CD.

CMS BIBLIOGRAPHY PAGE

A bibliography must be included at the end of the essay when using footnotes. All sources to be included—books, articles, web sites—are arranged alphabetically by the last names of the authors (or, if no author or editor is given, alphabetically by the title or other identifying word or phrase).

- Entries should have a hanging indent—all lines after the first line of each entry should be indented one-half inch from the left margin.
- Bibliography entries should be alphabetized by the last name of the first author of each work, and the author should be listed in last name, first name format.
- List entries for multiple articles by the same author in chronological order, from earliest to most recent.
- Include the complete title, maintaining the capitalization and punctuation used in the original title.
- Italicize titles of longer works, such as books and journals, and put quotes around the titles of shorter works, such as journal articles or essays in edited collections. Do not italicize or underline them.

Formatting Bibliography Entries

Books

Information to Include
- Full name(s) of author(s) or editor(s)
- Complete title (including subtitle) of book and edition, if not the first
- Publication information (city, publisher, date)
- Page reference for a chapter, essay, or other section of a book. Complete book sources do not include page numbers in the bibliography.
- DOI or URL for online books

One Author
Sedaris, David. *Barrel Fever*. New York: Little, Brown, 1994.

Two Works by the Same Author
To list two or more works by the same author in the bibliography, use three em-dashes followed by a period in place of the author name for each entry after the first.

Sedaris, David. *Barrel Fever*. New York: Little, Brown, 1994.

———. *Me Talk Pretty One Day*. New York: Little, Brown, 2000.

Two to Three Authors
Ward, Geoffrey, Ken Burns, and Kevin Baker. *Baseball: An Illustrated History*. New York: Alfred A. Knopf, Inc., 1996.

More than Three Authors
Barnes, Sonya et al. *Image Power: Top Image Experts Share What to Know to Look Your Best*. San Francisco: PowerDynamics Publishing, 2008.

Unknown Author
Beowulf. New York: Farrar, Straus and Giroux, 2000.

Author with an Editor
Fielding, Henry. *Tom Jones*, edited by Sheridan Baker. New York: W.W. Norton & Company, Inc., 1994.

Editor with no Author
Hart, Joseph, ed. *Che: The Life, Death, and Afterlife of a Revolutionary*. New York: Thunder's Mouth Press, 2003.

Author with a Translator
Gide, André. *Lafcadio's Adventures*. Translated by Dorothy Bussy. New York: Vintage Books, 1953.

Work in an Anthology
Bartholomae, David. "Inventing the University." In *When a Writer Can't Write*, edited by Mike Rose, 134–65. New York: Guilford, 1985.

Periodicals

Information to Include
- Full name(s) of author(s)
- Complete title (including subtitle) of article
- Title of periodical
- Volume number, issue number, date
- Page reference. Please note that if a page number is not available, a chapter or paragraph number or section header may be included.
- DOI or URL for online periodicals

Article in a Magazine
Miller, Jeremy. "The Tyranny of the Test: One Year as a Kaplan Coach in the Public Schools." *Harper's Magazine* September 2008.

Article in Journal Paginated by Issue
Because journals are paginated by issue, begin with page one for each issue and include the issue number in the citation.

Collins, Terence and Melissa Blum. "Meanness and Failure: Sanctioning Basic Writers." *Journal of Basic Writing* 19, no. 1 (2000): 13–21.

Article in Journal Paginated by Volume
Journals paginated by volume begin with page one in issue one, and page numbers continue in issue two where issue one left off. Therefore, it is not necessary to include an issue number.

Sledd, Andrew. "Readin' not Riotin': The Politics of Literacy." *College English* 50 (1998): 495–508.

Electronic Sources
Include all available relevant publication information, including the URL or, if available, the DOI.

Web Site
National Public Radio. *Morning Edition*. Accessed January 14, 2014. http://www.npr.org/programs/morning-edition.

Web Page
Abdullah, Mardziah Hayati. "The Impact of Electronic Communication on Writing." *ERIC Clearinghouse on Reading, English, and Communication*. http://www.ericdigests.org/2004-1/impact.htm.

Online Book

Austen, Jane. *Pride and Prejudice.* London, 1813. http://www.gutenberg. org/catalog/world/readfile?fk_files=3381939.

Article from an Online Periodical

Popular Magazine

Remnick, David. "Putin and the Exile." *New Yorker,* April 28, 2014, accessed April 28, 2014. http://www.newyorker.com/talk/comment/2014/04/ 28/140428taco_talk_remnick.

Scholarly Journal

Soliday, Mary. "From the Margins to the Mainstream: Reconceiving Remediation." *College Composition and Communication* 47, no. 1 (1996): 85–100. Accessed January 14, 2014. http://www.jstor.org/ stable/358275.

Video/Film

McGregor, Ewan, Albert Finney, Jessica Lange, Billy Crudup, and Marion Cotillard. *Big Fish.* DVD. Directed by Tim Burton. Culver City: Sony Home Pictures Entertainment, 2003.

Broadcast Program

Begin with the writer(s), followed by the name of the program in italics. Also include the director's name, broadcast date, distribution city and company, and publication medium (e.g., Television, Radio).

Door, Daniel, and Michael Schur. *Brooklyn Nine-Nine.* Directed by Ken Whittingham. 2014. Los Angeles: NBCUniversal Television Distribution.

Television Episode

Begin with the writer(s), followed by the name of episode in quotation marks and the program title in italics. Also include the season number, episode number, director's name, original broadcast date, distribution city and company, release date, and publication medium (e.g., Television, Radio).

Davis, Jeff, Dan Sworkin, and Jay Beattie, "Tabula Rasa." *Criminal Minds,* season 3, episode 19, directed by Steve Boyum, aired May 14, 2008. (Los Angeles: Paramount, 2010), DVD.

Sound Recording

List artist, title of album in italics, city and name of distribution company, medium, and date of original release.

Miranda, Lin-Manuel. *The Hamilton Mixtape.* New York: Atlantic Records, CD. Recorded 2016.

Student Style Manual for MLA, Chicago, and APA Documentation

APA Style

The *Publication Manual of the American Psychological Association*, or APA, is a style guide created by the American Psychological Association to establish formatting rules and bring consistency to their publications. Academic disciplines such as psychology, sociology, economics, business, and nursing, typically use APA style. The most recent publication, the 6th edition, was published in 2009 and updated in 2016.

APA Guidelines for Formatting Papers

- Start with a header that says "Running head:" followed immediately by a shortened version of the paper title in all caps, aligned to the left in the upper left corner of the page. On the same line, but aligned to the right of the page, will be "1" to indicate that the title page is your first page.

- Write your title again, this time centered in the upper half of the page and in title case, with the author's name centered below and then the author's institutional affiliation centered below that. In title case, upper-case letters begin each word with the exception of articles and prepositions.

- All of the text on the title page should be double spaced in a 12-point, easy-to-read font (such as Times New Roman).

- The essay should be typed, double spaced in 12-point, easy-to-read font (such as Times New Roman) on 8.5-inch by 11-inch paper, with 1-inch margins on all sides.

- Beginning with the second page, include the abbreviated title of your paper (50 characters max.) in all capital letters in a header aligned to the left. On the same line, but aligned right, include the page number.

- Change underlining to italics. However, some underlining may need to be preserved, depending on the original material.

APA Style

Running head: ABBREVIATED TITLE OF PAPER   1

Title of Paper

Your Name

Your College or University

Sample APA Title Page

- If your instructor requires you to include an abstract, which is commonly included in scholarly articles, the abstract will be on page 2 and will include the abbreviated title of your paper in all capital letters in a header aligned to the left. On the same line, but aligned right, include the page number. If you are not required to include an abstract, begin your paper on the second page.

- Fix commas and periods relative to quotation marks (commas and periods go inside the quotation marks, not outside: "Chapter 1," rather than "Chapter 1", for example).

- Use em dashes (—) and ellipses (…) where appropriate, and be consistent.

- Replace hyphens (-) with en dashes (–) where appropriate.

- The second printing of the 6th edition of the APA style guide recommends, but does not require, using two spaces after the end punctuation of a sentence, for ease of readability.

- The reference page should begin on a new page, separate from the essay.

APA GENERAL IN-TEXT CITATION RULES

- It is important to provide a lead-in to source quotations or paraphrases in the text, especially the first time the source is used. Lead-ins introduce the sources to the audience and provide a smooth transition to quotes and paraphrases within the text.

- While it is important to include page numbers when directly quoting from a source, you do not have to provide the page number when paraphrasing or summarizing an idea from a source. However, for pedagogical reasons, some professors will prefer that you include page numbers so it is always smart to ask in advance.

- Though authors writing in APA do not commonly reference the titles of works in their texts, if you do reference the title of a source in text:

  - Capitalize all words that are four letters long or more within the title of a source: *Pride and Prejudice*. Short words that are verbs, nouns, pronouns, adjectives, and adverbs are exceptions to this rule: *Everything Is Illuminated*, *Brave New World*.

  - Italicize the titles of longer works such as books, movies, anthologies, television series, or albums: *American Idol*; *Anchorman*. Put quotation marks around the titles of shorter works within the text, such as journal articles, essays in anthologies, and song titles: "Red"; "Inventing the University."

  - Capitalize both words in a hyphenated compound word: *The Tell-Tale Heart*. Also capitalize the first word after a colon or dash: *The World Is Flat: A Brief History of the Twenty-First Century*.

A Work by a Single Author

If quoting directly from a work, include the author, year of publication, and the page number (preceded by "p." for a single page or "pp." for multiple pages). When not directly quoting, exclude page numbers from the citation.

Sedaris (1994) recalls, "We rode round and round the block on our pony, who groaned beneath the collective weight of our rich and overwhelming capacity for love and understanding" (pp. 9–10).

"We rode round and round the block on our pony, who groaned beneath the collective weight of our rich and overwhelming capacity for love and understanding" (Sedaris, 1994, pp. 9–10).

Sedaris (1994) recalls circling his neighborhood atop his pony.

Block Quotations

Start quotations longer than 40 words on a new line, indented 1/2 inch from the left margin. Place the whole quote, double spaced, on the new margin. The parenthetical citation follows the end punctuation. Do not use quotation marks.

As a builder, Lubbers was tasked to determine the most effective method for ensuring the safety and integrity of structures in a variety of climates. Lubbers's (2013) study found the following:

> The prevailing wind being forecast for January 2 will be from the southwest, and will reach speeds of up to 50 miles per hour. This wind has the potential to cause significant damage to the current construction. The building should be braced heavily to avoid collapse. (p. 202)

Print Sources

Two Authors

List both authors whenever the work is cited. In the signal phrase, "and" should be used between the authors' names, while an ampersand (&) should be used in the parentheses.

Research by Collins and Blum (2000) outlines the way socioeconomics and politics outside the university also play a role in instigating the division between "basic" and "normal" writers (p. 14).

Researcher scholars outline the way socioeconomics and politics outside the university also play a role in instigating the division between "basic" and "normal" writers (Collins & Blum, 2000, p. 14).

Three to Five Authors
List all the authors by last name the first time the source is cited. In later citations, use the first author's last name followed by "et al." The et in et al. should not be followed by a period.

Ward, Burns, and Baker (1996) note, "The game varied from state to state, town to town, but town ball was the most popular" (p. 4).

(Ward et al., 1996, p. 4)

Six or More Authors
Use the first author's last name, followed by et al. You do not have to provide the page number when paraphrasing or summarizing from a source, but some professors will prefer that you do so; it is always smart to ask in advance.

Cincotta et al. (1994) assert that the launch of Sputnik expanded the competitive arena between the U.S. and the Soviet Union.

Unknown Author
If the author of a source is unknown, cite using the title in the lead-in, or include an abbreviated version of the title in the parenthetical citation.

A similar study determined that subjects lose time when switching from task to task ("Is Multitasking," 2001).

Authors with the Same Last Name
Include first initials with the last names to distinguish between the authors.

(R. Jones, 2012; A. Jones, 2003)

Anthology
According to David Bartholomae (1985), students who were less successful at this "invention" were considered basic writers; those who were more successful were not (p. 136).

Encyclopedia/Dictionary Entry
A citation is a "quotation from or reference to a book, paper, or author" (Citation, 2002).

APA Style

Indirect Sources

It may be necessary to use a work that has been cited in another source. Though it may seem strange, include the citations embedded within the original material you are quoting. You need not include the original work in your reference page unless you draw from the work elsewhere in your paper.

Young (2010) anticipates Fish's response, stating: "To this objection, Victor Villanueva, a Puerto Rican scholar of American studies, as well as language and literacy, point to 'writers of color who have been using the blended form [...] from the get-go' (351)" (p. 116).

Personal Interview/ Personal Communication

Personal communications are not included in the reference list. Cite the communicator's name, the phrase "personal communication," and the date of the communication parenthetically in your main text only.

Example

Danny Williams states that he and his colleagues experience tension when discussing personal issues (personal communication, June 14, 2017).

Electronic Sources

Web Sources

When possible, cite a web document the same as any other document.

Bianchi (2007) suggests [...]

If no author or date is given, cite using the title in the lead-in, or include an abbreviated version of the title in the parenthetical citation, and use the abbreviation "n.d." ("no date").

A similar study determined that subjects lost more time when switching from a familiar task to an unfamiliar task ("Is Multitasking," n.d.).

If you are directly quoting from the source and no page number is available for material you are directly quoting, include information that will help readers find the material being cited. If paragraphs are numbered, use "para." and follow with the paragraph number.

(Hubbard, 2014, para. 3).

Video/Film

Big Fish (2003), directed by Tim Burton, details the extraordinary life of Edward Bloom.

APA REFERENCE PAGE

The reference list, including all sources cited in the text, should appear on a separate page at the end of the text. The reference page should include the title "References" centered at the top of the page, with no bolding, underlining, italicizing, or quotation marks. All text in the reference section should be double spaced, with no additional spaces between entries.

- Entries should have a hanging indent—all lines after the first line of each entry should be indented one-half inch from the left margin.

- Reference list entries should be alphabetized by the last name of the first author of each work.

- For multiple articles by the same author, or authors listed in the same order, list the entries in chronological order, from earliest to most recent. In instances in which the same author has multiple works from the same year, list them in order from earliest to most recent with letters following the year (2017a, 2017b, and so on).

- Include the complete journal title in italics, maintaining the capitalization and punctuation used in the original. Include the volume and issue numbers (if applicable).

- When referring to books, chapters, articles, or web pages, capitalize only the first letter of the first word of a title and subtitle, the first word after a colon or a dash in the title, and proper nouns. Do not capitalize the first letter of the second word in a hyphenated compound word.

- Italicize titles of longer works (books, films); do not italicize, underline, or put quotes around the titles of shorter works (articles, songs).

Single Author
Use the last name, initials format. Note that the journal below is published annually, which means it has a volume number, but not an issue number.

Young, V. (2010). Should Writers Use They Own English? *Iowa Journal of Cultural Studies, 12*, 110–117.

Two Authors
List using the last name, initials format and use the ampersand (&) instead of "and."

Collins, T., & Blum, M. (2000). Meanness and failure: Sanctioning basic writers. *Journal of Basic Writing, 19*(1), 13–21.

Three to Seven Authors
Use the last name, initials format, separate authors' names using commas, and precede the final author's name with an ampersand.

Rubenstein, J., Meyer, D., & Evans, J. (2001). Executive control of cognitive processes in task switching. *Journal of Experimental Psychology: Human Perception and Performance, 27*(4), 763–797.

More Than Seven Authors

Follow the same rules as a source with three to seven authors, but after the sixth author's name, use an ellipses rather than listing authors' names. Then list the final author's name. In other words, there should not be more than seven names listed in the citation.

Barnes, S., Buchanan, W., Chenn, H., Elrick, H., Graham, J. A., King, D....
 Law, K. (2008). Web site usability for the blind and low-vision user. In
 Image power: Top image experts share what to know to look your best.
 San Francisco, CA: PowerDynamics Publishing.

Two or More Works by the Same Author

Use the last name, initials format for all entries and list the entries by the year, earliest first.

Child, L. (2007).

Child, L. (2010).

Unknown Author

When a source does not include an author's name, use the source's title (abbreviated, if the title is long) rather than an author's name.

Beowulf. (2000). New York, NY: Farrar, Straus and Giroux.

Books

For the publication location information, include the city and the two-letter state abbreviation (New York, NY).

Basic Format for Books

Sedaris, D. (1994). *Barrel fever.* New York, NY: Little, Brown.

Author with an Editor

Fielding, H. (1973). *Tom Jones.* S. Baker (Ed.). New York, NY: W. W. Norton
 & Company, Inc.

Editor as Author

Hart, J. (Ed.). (2003). *Che: The life, death, and afterlife of a revolutionary.*
 New York, NY: Thunder's Mouth Press.

Author with a Translator

Gide, A. (1953). *Lafcadio's adventures.* (D. Bussy, Trans.). New York, NY:
 Vintage Books. (Original work published 1914).

Work in an Anthology

Bartholomae, D. (1985). Inventing the university. In M. Rose (Ed.), *When a
 writer can't write* (pp. 134–165). New York, NY: Guilford.

Encyclopedia/Dictionary Entry

Citation. (2002). In *The shorter Oxford English dictionary* (5th ed.). Oxford, UK: Oxford University Press.

Periodicals

Authors are listed in last name, initial format, followed by the publication year in parentheses. The title of the article is in sentence case (only the first word and proper nouns are capitalized). The title of the periodical is in title case and is followed by the volume number, both of which are in italics.

Article in a Magazine

Miller, J. (2008, September 2). The tyranny of the test: One year as a Kaplan coach in the public schools. *Harper's Magazine,* 35–46.

Article in a Newspaper

Precede page numbers with p. (for a single page) or pp. (for more than one page).

Timson, J. (2001, August 7). Stop all that multitasking, study suggests. *The Toronto Star,* p. E2.

Article in Journal Paginated by Issue

Because journals paginated by issue begin with page one for each issue, the issue number is included in the citation. The parentheses and issue number are not italicized or underlined.

Collins. T. & Blum, M. (2000). Meanness and failure: Sanctioning basic writers. *Journal of Basic Writing, 19*(1), 13–21.

Article in Journal Paginated by Volume

Journals paginated by volume begin with page one in issue one, and page numbers continue in issue two where issue one left off. Therefore, it is not necessary to include an issue number.

Sledd, A. (1998). Readin' not riotin': The politics of literacy. *College English, 50,* 495–508.

Electronic Sources

Follow the same guidelines as printed articles, and include all available relevant information. Because web sites are often updated and the same information may not be available later, the DOI should be used rather than the URL whenever possible.

Web Site

National Public Radio. (2014, January). *Morning edition.* Retrieved from NPR web site http://www.npr.org/programs/morning-edition/

Web Page

Abdullah, M. H. (2004, October). The impact of electronic communication on writing. *ERIC Clearinghouse on Reading, English, and Communication.* Retrieved from http://www.ericdigests.org/2004-1/impact.htm

Online Book

Austen, J. (1813). *Pride and prejudice.* Retrieved from http://www.gutenberg. org/catalog/world/readfile?fk_files=3381939

Article from an Online Magazine

Remnick, D. (2014, April 28). Putin and the exile. *New Yorker.* Retrieved from http://www.newyorker.com/talk/comment/2014/04/28/140428taco_ talk_remnick

Article from an Online Periodical

Soliday, M. (1996). From the margins to the mainstream: Reconceiving remediation. *College Composition and Communication, 47*(1). Retrieved from http://www.jstor.org/stable/358275

Video/Film

Cohen, B., Zanuck, R. & Jinks, D. (Producers), & Burton, T. (Director). (2003). *Big fish* [Motion picture]. USA: Sony Home Pictures Entertainment.

Broadcast Program

Goor, D. & Schur, M. (Writers), & Whittingham, K. (Director). (2014, March 19). Unsolvable. *Brooklyn nine-nine.* [Television series]. In D. Goor & M. Schur (Producers). Los Angeles, CA: NBCUniversal Television Distribution.

Television Episode

Davis, J., Sworkin, D., & Beattie, J. (Writers), & Boyum, S. (Director). (2008). Tabula rasa [Television series episode]. In E.A. Bernero (Producer), *Criminal minds.* Los Angeles, CA: Paramount.

Music or Sound Recording

Miranda, L. (2016). *Hamilton Mixtape* [CD]. New York, NY: Atlantic Records.

Student Style Manual for MLA, Chicago, and APA Documentation

Citation Chart

	In-Text Citations
	Print Sources
	Author Named in a Signal Phrase
MLA	Sedaris recalls, "We rode round and round the block on our pony, who groaned beneath the collective weight of our rich and overwhelming capacity for love and understanding" (9–10).
CMS	Sedaris recalls, "We rode round and round the block on our pony, who groaned beneath the collective weight of our rich and overwhelming capacity for love and understanding."[1] 1. David Sedaris, *Barrel Fever* (New York: Little, Brown, 1994), 9–10.
APA	Sedaris (1994) recalls, "We rode round and round the block on our pony, who groaned beneath the collective weight of our rich and overwhelming capacity for love and understanding" (pp. 9–10).
	Author Not Named in a Signal Phrase
MLA	He states, "We rode round and round the block on our pony, who groaned beneath the collective weight of our rich and overwhelming capacity for love and understanding" (Sedaris 9–10).
CMS	He states, "We rode round and round the block on our pony, who groaned beneath the collective weight of our rich and overwhelming capacity for love and understanding."[1] 1. David Sedaris, *Barrel Fever* (New York: Little, Brown, 1994), 9–10.
APA	He states, "We rode round and round the block on our pony, who groaned beneath the collective weight of our rich and overwhelming capacity for love and understanding" (Sedaris, 1994, pp. 9–10).

Citation Chart

In-Text Citations		
Two or Three Authors		
MLA	Collins and Blum outline the way socioeconomics and politics outside the university also play a role in instigating the division between "basic" and "normal" writers (14).	
	The authors outline the way socioeconomics and politics outside the university also play a role in instigating the division between "basic" and "normal" writers (Collins and Blum 14).	
CMS	Collins and Blum outline the way socioeconomics and politics outside the university also play a role in instigating the division between "basic" and "normal" writers.[3]	
	3. Collins and Blum, "Meanness and Failure," 14.	
APA	Research by Collins and Blum (2000) outlines the way socioeconomics and politics outside the university also play a role in instigating the division between "basic" and "normal" writers (p. 14).	
More Than Three Authors		
MLA	Cincotta et al. assert that the launch of Sputnik expanded the competitive arena between the U.S. and the Soviet Union (68).	
	Historians assert that the launch of Sputnik expanded the competitive arena between the U.S. and the Soviet Union (Cincotta et al. 68).	
	Cincotta, Brown, Burant, Green, Holden, and Marshall assert that the launch of Sputnik expanded the competitive arena between the U.S. and the Soviet Union (68).	
CMS	Cincotta et al. assert that the launch of Sputnik expanded the competitive arena between the U.S. and the Soviet Union.[2]	
	2. Howard Cincotta et al., *An Outline of American History* (Washington D.C.: United States Information Agency, 1994).	
APA	For the first use in text, list all author names:	
	Cincotta, Brown, Burant, Green, Holden, and Marshall (1994) [...]	
	For subsequent entries, use et al.:	
	Cincotta et al. (1994) assert that the launch of Sputnik expanded the competitive arena between the U.S. and the Soviet Union.	
Unknown Author		
MLA	A study determined that subjects lose time when switching from task to task ("Is Multitasking" 3).	
CMS	A study determined that subjects lose time when switching from task to task.[4]	
	Short citation:	
	4. "Is Multitasking," 3.	
APA	A similar study determined that subjects lose time when switching from task to task ("Is Multitasking," 2001, p. 3).	

	In-Text Citations
	Work in an Anthology
MLA	According to David Bartholomae, students who were less successful at this "invention" were considered basic writers; those who were more successful were not (136).
CMS	According to David Bartholomae, students who were less successful at this "invention" were considered basic writers; those who were more successful were not.[6] 6. David Bartholomae, "Inventing the University," in *When a Writer Can't Write*, ed. Mike Rose (New York: Guilford, 1985). 134–65.
APA	According to David Bartholomae (1985), students who were less successful at this "invention" were considered basic writers; those who were more successful were not (p. 136).
	Encyclopedia/Dictionary
MLA	A citation is a "quotation from or reference to a book, paper, or author" ("Citation").
CMS	A citation is a "quotation from or reference to a book, paper, or author."[10] **Use footnote only; does not appear in bibliography.** 10. *The Shorter Oxford English Dictionary*, 5th ed., s.v. "citation."
APA	A citation is a "quotation from or reference to a book, paper, or author" (Citation, 2002).
	Electronic Sources
	Web Sources
MLA	For electronic sources, include the first item (author name, title, etc.) in the Works Cited entry that corresponds to the citation. Do not include URLs in the text unless absolutely necessary; if included, make the URL as brief as possible, such as npr.org rather than http://www.npr.org.
CMS	When possible, follow the same guidelines for printed materials. Include all available information, including the URL or, if available, the digital object identifier (DOI), and use the long footnote citation format.
APA	When possible, cite a web document the same as any other document. If no author or date is given, cite using the title in the lead-in, or include an abbreviated version of the title in the parenthetical citation, and use the abbreviation "n.d." ("no date"). If no page number is available and you are quoting from the source, include information that will help readers find the material being cited. If paragraphs are numbered, use "para." and follow with the paragraph number.

Citation Chart

In-Text Citations	
Film	
MLA	*Big Fish*, directed by Tim Burton, details the extraordinary life of Edward Bloom (2003).
CMS	*Big Fish*, directed by Tim Burton, details the extraordinary life of Edward Bloom.[15] 15. *Big Fish*, directed by Tim Burton (2003; Culver City, CA: Sony Home Pictures Entertainment, 2004), DVD.
APA	*Big Fish* (2003), directed by Tim Burton, details the extraordinary life of Edward Bloom.

End-of-Text Citations		
Books		
General Book Format		
MLA **Works Cited**	Sedaris, David. *Barrel Fever*. Little, Brown, 1994.	
CMS **Bibliography**	Sedaris, David. *Barrel Fever*. New York: Little, Brown, 1994.	
APA **References**	Sedaris, D. (1994). *Barrel fever*. New York, NY: Little, Brown.	
Two or Three Authors		
MLA	Ward, Geoffrey, Ken Burns, and Kevin Baker. *Baseball: An Illustrated History*. Alfred A. Knopf, Inc. 1996.	
CMS	Ward, Geoffrey, Ken Burns, and Kevin Baker. *Baseball: An Illustrated History*. New York: Alfred A. Knopf, Inc., 1996.	
APA	Ward, G., Burns, K., & Baker, K. (1996). *Baseball: An illustrated history*. New York: Alfred A Knopf, Inc.	
More Than Three Authors		
MLA	Barnes, Sonya, et al. [...]	
CMS	Barnes, Sonya et al. [...]	
APA	Three to seven authors: Rubenstein, J., Meyer, D., & Evans, J. (2001). [...] More than seven authors: Barnes, S., Buchanan, W., Chenn, H., Elrick, H., Graham, J. A., King, D....Law, K. (2008). [...]	
Unknown Author		
MLA	*Beowulf*. Farrar, Straus and Giroux, 2000.	
CMS	*Beowulf*. New York: Farrar, Straus and Giroux, 2000.	
APA	*Beowulf*. (2000). New York, NY: Farrar, Straus and Giroux.	
Author with an Editor		
MLA	Fielding, Henry. *Tom Jones*. Edited by Sheridan Baker, [...]	
CMS	Fielding, Henry. *Tom Jones*, edited by Sheridan Baker. [...]	
APA	Fielding, H. (1973). *Tom Jones*. S. Baker (Ed.). [...]	

Citation Chart

Citation Chart

End-of-Text Citations	
Editor with no Author	
MLA	*Impossibly Funky: A* Cashiers du Cinemart *Collection.* Edited by M. White, [...]
CMS	White, M., ed. [...]
APA	White, M. (Ed.). (2010). *Impossibly funky: A* Cashiers du Cinemart *collection.* [...]
Author with a Translator	
MLA	Gide, André. *Lafcadio's Adventures.* Translated by Dorothy Bussy, [...]
CMS	Gide, André. *Lafcadio's Adventures.* Translated by Dorothy Bussy. [...]
APA	Gide, A. (1953). *Lafcadio's adventures.* (D. Bussy, Trans.). [...]
Work in an Anthology	
MLA	Bartholomae, David. "Inventing the University." *When a Writer Can't Write*, edited by Mike Rose, Guilford, 1985, pp. 134–65.
CMS	Bartholomae, David. "Inventing the University." In *When a Writer Can't Write*, edited by Mike Rose, 134–65. New York: Guilford, 1985.
APA	Bartholomae, D. (1985). Inventing the university. In M. Rose (Ed.), *When a writer can't write* (pp. 134–165). New York: Guilford.
Encyclopedia/Dictionary Entry	
MLA	"Citation." *The Shorter Oxford English Dictionary.* 5th ed., 2002.
CMS	**In footnotes only.**
APA	Citation. (2002). In *The shorter Oxford English dictionary.* (5th ed.). [...]
Articles in Periodicals	
Magazine	
MLA	Miller, Jeremy. "The Tyranny of the Test: One Year as a Kaplan Coach in the Public Schools." *Harper's Magazine*, 2 Sept. 2008, pp. 35–46.
CMS	Miller, Jeremy. "The Tyranny of the Test: One Year as a Kaplan Coach in the Public Schools." *Harper's Magazine* September 2008.
APA	Miller, J. (2008, September 2). The tyranny of the test: One year as a Kaplan coach in the public schools. *Harper's Magazine*, 35–46.

	End-of-Text Citations
	Newspaper
MLA	Timson, Judith. "Stop All That Multitasking, Study Suggests." *The Toronto Star*, 7 Aug. 2001, p. E2.
CMS	**In footnotes only.**
APA	Timson, J. (2001, August 7). Stop all that multitasking, study suggests. *The Toronto Star*, p. E2.
	Journal
MLA	Collins, Terence, and Melissa Blum. "Meanness and Failure: Sanctioning Basic Writers." *Journal of Basic Writing*, vol. 19, no. 1, 2000, pp. 13–21.
CMS	Collins, Terence and Melissa Blum. "Meanness and Failure: Sanctioning Basic Writers." *Journal of Basic Writing* 19, no. 1 (2000): 13–21.
APA	Collins, T. & Blum, M. (2000). Meanness and failure: Sanctioning basic writers. *Journal of Basic Writing, 19*(1), 13–21.
	Electronic Sources
	Entire Web Site
MLA	National Public Radio. *Morning Edition*. NPR, 14 January 2014, www.npr.org/programs/morning-edition. Accessed 14 Jan. 2014.
CMS	National Public Radio. *Morning Edition*. Accessed January 14, 2014. http://www.npr.org/programs/morning-edition.
APA	National Public Radio. (2014, January). *Morning edition*. Retrieved from NPR web site http://www.npr.org/programs/morning-edition/
	Page from a Web Site
MLA	Abdullah, Mardziah Hayati. "The Impact of Electronic Communication on Writing." *EricDigests.org*. ERIC Clearinghouse on Reading, English, and Communication, 2003, www.ericdigests.org/2004-1/impact.htm. Accessed 13 Oct. 2004.
CMS	Abdullah, Mardziah Hayati. "The Impact of Electronic Communication on Writing." *ERIC Clearinghouse on Reading, English, and Communication*. http://www.ericdigests.org/2004-1/impact.htm.
APA	Abdullah, M. H. (2004, October). The impact of electronic communication on writing. *ERIC Clearinghouse on Reading, English, and Communication*. Retrieved from http://www.ericdigests.org/2004-1/impact.htm

Citation Chart

End-of-Text Citations	
Online Book	
MLA	Austen, Jane. *Pride and Prejudice*. Project Gutenberg, 2013, www. gutenberg.org/catalog/world/readfile?fk_files=3381939. Accessed 14 Apr. 2014.
CMS	Austen, Jane. *Pride and Prejudice*. London, 1813. http://www. gutenberg.org/catalog/world/readfile?fk_files=3381939.
APA	Austen, J. (1813). *Pride and prejudice*. Project Gutenberg. Retrieved from http://www.gutenberg.org/catalog/world/ readfile?fk_files=3381939
Article in an Online Magazine/Newspaper	
MLA	Remnick, David. "Putin and the Exile." *New Yorker*. NewYorker.com, 28 Apr. 2014, www.newyorker.com/talk/comment/2014/04/28/ 140428taco_talk_remnick. Accessed 28 Apr. 2014.
CMS	Remnick, David. "Putin and the Exile." *New Yorker*, April 28, 2014, accessed April 28, 2014. http://www.newyorker.com/talk/ comment/2014/04/28/140428taco_talk_remnick.
APA	Remnick, D. (2014, April 28). Putin and the exile. *New Yorker*. Retrieved from http://www.newyorker.com/talk/ comment/2014/04/28/140428taco_talk_remnick
Article in an Online Journal	
MLA	Soliday, Mary. "From the Margins to the Mainstream: Reconceiving Remediation." *College Composition and Communication*, vol. 47, no. 1, 1996, pp. 85–100, www.jstor.org/stable/358275. Accessed 14 Jan. 2014.
CMS	Soliday, Mary. "From the Margins to the Mainstream: Reconceiving Remediation." *College Composition and Communication* 47, no. 1 (1996): 85–100. Accessed January 14, 2014. http://www.jstor. org/stable/358275.
APA	Soliday, M. (1996). From the margins to the mainstream: Reconceiving remediation. *College Composition and Communication, 47*(1). Retrieved from http://www.jstor.org/ stable/358275

End-of-Text Citations	
Film	
MLA	*Big Fish*. Directed by Tim Burton, performances by Ewan McGregor, Albert Finney, Jessica Lange, Billy Crudup, and Marion Cotillard, Columbia, 2003.
CMS	McGregor, Ewan, Albert Finney, Jessica Lange, Billy Crudup, and Marion Cotillard. *Big Fish*. DVD. Directed by Tim Burton. Culver City: Sony Home Pictures Entertainment, 2004.
APA	Cohen, B., Zanuck, R. & Jinks, D. (Producer), & Burton, T. (Director). (2003). *Big fish* [Motion picture]. USA: Sony Home Pictures Entertainment.
Television Program	
MLA	"Tabula Rasa." *Criminal Minds: Season 3*, written by Jeff Davis, Dan Sworkin, and Jay Beattie, directed by Steve Boyum, Paramount, 2010.
CMS	Davis, Jeff, Dan Sworkin, and Jay Beattie, "Tabula Rasa." *Criminal Minds*, season 3, episode 19, directed by Steve Boyum, aired May 14, 2008. (Los Angeles: Paramount, 2010), DVD.
APA	Davis, J., Sworkin, D., & Beattie, J. (Writers) & Boyum, S. (Director). (2008). Tabula rasa [Television series episode]. In E.A. Bernero (Producer), *Criminal minds*. Los Angeles, CA: Paramount.
Sound Recording	
MLA	Miranda, Lin-Manuel. *The Hamilton Mixtape*, Atlantic Records, 2016.
CMS	Miranda, Lin-Manuel. *The Hamilton Mixtape*. New York: Atlantic Records, CD. Recorded 2016.
APA	Miranda, L. (2016). *Hamilton Mixtape* [CD]. New York, NY: Atlantic Records.

Sample Papers in MLA, Chicago, and APA Styles

Sample Papers in Different Styles

In this section we provide you with examples of argumentative papers in three different formatting and documentation styles, APA (American Psychological Association), MLA (Modern Language Association), and CMS (Chicago Manual of Style). The goal is not only to provide you with models for citation in the different styles, but also to demonstrate the rhetorical and stylistic conventions of each. As you read through the samples, take time to notice the nuances of each style. Ask yourself how the varied parenthetical citations affect your reading. How does the use of footnotes allow the author to present information? Why are dates used in parenthetical citations in APA, but not in MLA? How do the requirements of each style represent what the field values most? Keep in mind that the conventions of each style were decided on by a board of experts in the field who believe that the current models (i.e., APA 6, CMS 6, MLA 8) are the best ways for research in their disciplines to be presented to readers. As you become more familiar with documentation styles, ask yourself if you agree with their choices.

• •

> WRITE a list of the courses you've taken so far in college.
> Which formatting and documentation style was used in
> each? Or, if you didn't write a paper in the course, which
> style is most commonly associated with the discipline?
> In which field and/or style do you feel most comfortable
> writing and why?

• •

AMBER HATCHER

Amber Hatcher is a sophomore at Arkansas State University from Trumann, AR. When she is not in class or working, she enjoys reading, writing, and spending time with her husband.

Ever since she was four years old, she knew that her purpose in life was to write. She loves writing, not only to escape this world herself, but to let others escape as well. A quote from the Harry Potter character, Albus Dumbledore best describes how she feels about writing: "Words are, in my not-so-humble opinion, our most inexhaustible source of magic."

THE ASSIGNMENT: ARGUMENTATIVE ESSAY

An argumentative essay is a formal piece in which the student demonstrates the ability to present a strong argument with attention to the rhetorical appeals, acknowledgement of and response to counterargument, and the ability to select, evaluate, and incorporate sources alongside original ideas.

This type of essay can cover anything from local or national politics, to views on pop culture, or issues currently in public discussion, but it also requires the author to go in search of evidence to support his or her views. This use of outside sources and research should strengthen and enhance the author's position. An author should also investigate and discuss the views which oppose his or her argument, as this will bring clarity and a well-roundedness to the paper that allows the reader to judge the strength of the author's thesis.

Sample Essay in MLA Style (8th Edition)

Amber Hatcher

Written for Geoffrey Clegg's Composition II Course
· ·

Hatcher 1

Amber Hatcher

Mr. Clegg

ENG 1013

November 12, 2014

Muggles and Mudbloods and Creatures, Oh My!

Racism in the Wizarding World

Racism has been a major problem in society for centuries. As a result, it has become a key theme in various works of literature, including the *Harry Potter* series. J.K. Rowling gives a clear insight into how racism has affected the world of humans by illustrating it through a world of magic. She divides the racism in the wizarding world into three major categories throughout the series.

The first category concerning racism in the *Harry Potter* series is the distinction between purebloods and non-purebloods. Lord Voldemort belonged to the Slytherin House while he attended Hogwarts School of Witchcraft and Wizardry. Out of all four houses (Gryffindor, Hufflepuff, Ravenclaw, and Slytherin), Slytherin housed several students who turned evil. The founder of the Slytherin House, Salazar Slytherin, only wanted pureblood students to attend Hogwarts. He did not think half-bloods or Muggle-borns were worthy enough to attend. He was outnumbered, however, as the other founders disagreed. Salazar Slytherin then built the Chamber of Secrets, killing students who were not pureblood. The other founders quickly discovered it, closing the Chamber and banishing Salazar Slytherin from Hogwarts. Years later, Tom Riddle, Salazar Slytherin's heir, reopened the Chamber and continued his legacy.

Sample Papers in MLA, Chicago, and APA Styles

Hatcher 2

J.K. Rowling compares Lord Voldemort to Hitler. Both believed in racial purity, although they themselves were not what they believed to be pure. Hitler had Jewish blood, and Tom Riddle was a half-blood. Because of this, their killing people of their own blood "might have been an attempt to eliminate the part of himself he loathed" (Whited 3). She also says that the reopening of the Chamber "coincides with the opening of the Nazis' death chambers" (Whited 3). Racism transpired to the modern times of the wizarding world but not to the same extent, at first. Although the Chamber was once again reopened by Tom Riddle, racism dealt more with verbal abuse. This can be seen by Draco Malfoy's constant comments towards Hermione Granger, such as when he called her a "filthy little Mudblood" (*Chamber of Secrets* 112), which is a cruel name pureblood wizards use to describe Muggle-borns. It can also be seen by the portrait of Mrs. Black, Sirius' mother, who shouts obscenities like, "FILTHY HALF-BREEDS, BESMIRCHING THE HOUSE OF MY FATHERS" (*Order of the Phoenix* 179) and "MUDBLOODS! SCUM! CREATURES OF DIRT!" (*Order of the Phoenix* 180) whenever the Order of the Phoenix meets at Number Twelve, Grimmauld Place. However, after Dumbledore's death, Voldemort's followers, the Death Eaters, took over. The Ministry of Magic was going through drastic changes, including the addition of a new department called the "Muggle-Born Registration Commission." The proceedings to determine whether a witch or wizard was a Muggle-born were very much like the Salem Witch Trials. A witch or wizard would be accused of being a Muggle-born, even if they were half-bloods. At the hearing of Mary Cattermole, Yaxley, the new Minister of Magic, states, "The brats of Mudbloods do not stir our sympathies" (*Deathly Hallows* 259), and Dolores Umbridge tells her, "Wands only choose witches or wizards. You are not a witch" (*Deathly Hallows* 261). If any witch or wizard had Muggles in their family, they were registered as a Muggle-born.

The next manner of racism in the wizarding world is between wizards and magical creatures. There are several wizards who are kind to the magical beings (house-elves, werewolves, etc.), but there are others who treat them as though they are nothing. During the times of slavery in America, slaves were not viewed as equals. This is also the case for house-elves. Dobby, a house-elf, is a slave to the Malfoys. When Dobby arrives at the Dursley's, Harry suggests that Dobby sit down. Dobby bursts into to tears, stating, "Dobby has *never* been asked to sit down by a wizard—like an equal" (*Chamber of Secrets* 13). Also like the slaves, house-elves are beaten whenever they do something wrong. Dobby tells Harry, "Dobby is always having to punish himself for something…Sometimes they reminds me to do extra punishments" (*Chamber of Secret*s 14).

Some wizards did not like werewolves or giants. In *Prisoner of Azkaban*, the first werewolf in the series is introduced as the new Defense Against the Dark Arts professor, Remus Lupin. While talking to Harry in the Shrieking Shack, he tells him that "other parents weren't likely to want their children exposed to me" (*Prisoner of Azkaban* 353). He also tells Harry "I have been shunned all my adult life, unable to find paid work because of what I am" (*Prisoner of Azkaban* 356). Even though he stayed away from people during the one week a month when he turned into a werewolf and started taking the Wolfsbane Potion so he could still have his human thoughts, people still feared him. Dolores Umbridge is one of the more racist wizards concerning magical creatures, which is seen when she calls the centaurs "Filthy half-breeds!...Beasts! Uncontrolled animals!" (*Order of the Phoenix* 755). These magical creatures are part-human or have human characteristics, but because they are a different race than the majority of wizards, they are prejudiced against them.

The third and final type of racism in the *Harry Potter* series is between wizards and Muggles. Wizards know that Muggles exist, but "only a very

Hatcher 4

limited number of Muggles know about Wizards"[1] (Bertilsson 5). The ones that do typically consider them strange or fear them. The Dursleys are one of the groups of Muggles that hate wizards. This is why they ignore anything unusual and try to keep Harry from attending Hogwarts. Whenever they took him in, they "had hoped that if they kept Harry as downtrodden as possible, they would be able to squash the magic out of him" (*Prisoner of Azkaban* 2). Their attempts were unsuccessful, however. When Harry first received his acceptance letter into Hogwarts, Vernon tells Petunia, "I'm not having one in the house, Petunia! Didn't we swear when we took him in we'd stamp out this dangerous nonsense?" (*Sorcerer's Stone* 36). Harry cannot even say the word "magic" in their house without being yelled at. When Uncle Vernon tells Harry to give him a pan, Harry asks for the magic word. Uncle Vernon becomes angry, yelling "WHAT HAVE I TOLD YOU ABOUT SAYING THE 'M' WORD IN OUR HOUSE?" and "I WILL NOT TOLERATE MENTION OF YOUR ABNORMALITY UNDER THIS ROOF!" (*Chamber of Secrets* 2).

Some wizards, like Mr. Weasley, who works for the Misuse of Muggle Artifacts department in the Ministry of Magic, find Muggles fascinating. Other wizards, such as the Malfoys, look down upon Muggles and upon those wizards who think there is nothing wrong with Muggles. Lucius Malfoy looks pointedly at Hermione's parents after Mr. Weasley states, "We have a very different idea of what disgraces the name of wizard" (*Chamber of Secrets* 62). Then, while talking about Mr. Weasley, Pius Thicknesse says, "If you ask me, the blood traitors are as bad as the Mudbloods" (*Deathly Hallows* 247). This goes back to the concept of Slytherins only believing that purebloods should be allowed an education at Hogwarts.

The same problems that were seen in our world during the Holocaust and during the times of slavery are also seen in J.K. Rowling's *Harry Potter*

---

1   Notice that "Wizards" is capitalized in this instance because it is capitalized in the article (Ed.).

book series. Although Muggles and wizards are both human, and although non-purebloods and magical creatures share the same magical powers as wizards, they are looked down upon in the wizarding world. They are not seen as equals by many, even though they make up the majority of the population. J.K. Rowling reminds us that racism is still a problem today through her unforgettable world of characters.

However, some people suggest that J.K. Rowling is a racist herself. The main support for this claim is the fact that the majority of the characters in the *Harry Potter* series are white. According to a 2001 census of the United Kingdom, where the series takes place, "it puts the total of white people in the UK at 92.14%" (Adam). Harry would have graduated a few years before this, so it makes sense that white people form the bulk of the student body and staff. However, that is not the problem. The problem is that the characters who are of a different race are only minor characters. Take Dean Thomas and Angelina Johnson, for instance. They are both black students, but barely get any recognition. Angelina Johnson is only referred to when talking about Quidditch, the wizarding sport, and Dean is best known as his role as Ginny Weasley's boyfriend before she finally ends up with Harry.

Another character is Cho Chang. She first appears in *Harry Potter and the Goblet of Fire*, when Harry develops a crush on her. They are together briefly in the next book, *Harry Potter and the Order of the Phoenix*. Rachel Rostad, a poet, rants in her video "To J.K. Rowling, From Cho Chang" about four things. The first thing she rants about is how the non-white characters do not develop throughout the story. She even goes so far as to call the character "worthless" ("Rachel Rostad..."). The second is the way J.K. Rowling stereotyped Cho Chang. Most of the time, when someone hears the word "Asian," they automatically think of the word "nerd." At Hogwarts, the "nerdy" house is Ravenclaw, which coincidentally is the house that Cho Chang belongs to. The next point she brings up is the fact that students of other races make up a minority and that those students are only minor

Hatcher 6

characters in the series whereas the main characters are white. In the video, she states "Between me, Dean, and the Indian twins, Hogwarts has like... five brown people? It doesn't matter we're all minor characters. Nah, you're not racist!" ("Rachel Rostad..."). The last thing she rants about is her name. Cho Chang is a Chinese character whose name is made up of two Korean last names. Rachel Rostad compares this to "a Frenchman being named 'Garcia Sanchez'" ("Rachel Rostad..."). However, this is untrue as "Chang" is actually one of the fifty most common Chinese surnames. Additionally, it is not a fault in the story that the character wasn't developed. Rowling only developed the characters who were essential to the plot. Sure, Cho Chang could have been more developed, but she was only Harry's love interest for two out of seven of the books, so why would she have been?

One more character is often brought up when people start debating whether or not J.K. Rowling is racist. That character is Lavender Brown. In the first few films, where her character is of little significance, she is portrayed as black. Then, comes *Harry Potter and the Half-Blood Prince*. In that book/film, she becomes Ron Weasley's girlfriend. However, she is no longer black. Instead, she is played by a white actress. This does not necessarily mean that J.K. Rowling is racist. If anybody could be considered racist in this situation, it would be the person who selects the cast, because Rowling is not in charge of that, but that is only the case if the casting director did not actually want Lavender to be black. Since interracial relationships are typically looked down upon in today's society, that is semi-understandable. Most of the interracial relationships in movies I have seen are abusive, where the black boyfriend beats up his white girlfriend and goes to jail. Movies like those show interracial relationships in a negative way, corrupting a lot of minds into thinking that they are wrong. So, is that why Lavender Brown jumps from being black to white? Another, more plausible, explanation would just be that they needed a replacement. Maybe the actress that had played her in the first few movies just did not want to be her anymore, and the casting directors held auditions for a new Lavender. In situations like these, people tend to jump for the racist card rather than thinking through it rationally.

None of these characters make J.K. Rowling a racist. She was trying to create a semi-realistic aspect to her fantasy world. She made most of the students attending Hogwarts white, because the majority of the United Kingdom is white. She did not develop the minor characters because they weren't a part of the bigger picture, not just because they weren't white. That is a pure coincidence. In her novels, she doesn't state whether Lavender is black or white; the casting directors chose the actresses to play her in the movies for any variety of possible reasons.

What J.K. Rowling did was make the wizarding world as realistic as possible by combining fiction with reality. She created an entire fantasy world based on her imagination but integrated so many aspects of the world around her that it came to life for the reader. No one paid attention to the fact that non-white characters were minor characters. They were more interested in the story. As people reread the books as they get older, they notice the race issues that she so cleverly hid in them. She shows us how terrible racism can be in our own world by illustrating how disastrous it is in the wizarding world.

Hatcher 8

Works Cited

Adam. "Did you know Harry Potter was racist." *WordPress*, 21 April 2013, xdind.com/did-you-know-harry-potter-was-racist/.

Bertilsson, Andreas. "Freaks and Muggles: Intolerance and prejudice in *Harry Potter and the Philosopher's Stone*." Kristianstad U., 2007, pp. 3–17.

"Rachel Rostad—'To JK Rowling, from Cho Chang' (CUPSI 2013 Finals)." *YouTube*, uploaded by Button Poetry, 13 April 2013, www.youtube .com/watch?v=iFPWwx96Kew.

Rowling, J.K. *Harry Potter and the Sorcerer's Stone.* Scholastic, 1998.

---. *Harry Potter and the Chamber of Secrets.* Scholastic, 1999.

---. *Harry Potter and the Prisoner of Azkaban.* Scholastic, 1999.

---. *Harry Potter and the Order of the Phoenix.* Scholastic, 2003.

---. *Harry Potter and the Deathly Hallows.* Scholastic, 2007.

Whited, Lana. "1492, 1942, 1992: The Theme of Race in the Harry Potter Series." *The Looking Glass: New Perspectives on Children's Literature*, vol. 10, no. 1, 2006, pp. 1–7.

• •

Note: When inputting URLs in MLA 8 you use the entire web address, with the exception of "http://."

• •

WILLIAM KAZYAK

William Kazyak was born in Baltimore, MD, but considers his hometown to be Manila, AR. He is an Arkansas State University Piano Performance Major who enjoys playing the piano, listening to classical music and early pop/rock, like the Beach Boys, building model airplanes, and learning about the military. He also enjoys playing sports and running.

Though Kazyak has not always enjoyed writing, he explains, "There have been plenty of times in which what I wanted to say seemed to simply flow out onto the paper. I enjoy being able to put my thoughts down in an orderly manner and being able to refer back to them later."

Kazyak's advice to Composition I and II students? "Good, thoughtful writing takes time—it is not something that can be rushed." He further advises his peers: "Plan the work! Spread it out over time so you are not rushing at the end, and organize it thoughtfully, with smooth transitions from one idea to the next. Take advantage of spare time such as weekends or breaks to think through the assignment and what you want to say."

THE ASSIGNMENT: RESEARCH PAPER

Consider a topic about which you would like to learn more. This topic can be anything, as long as it is a topic appropriate for scholarly inquiry. Students in the past have chosen an historical event, a social or cultural issue, or a scientific theory. Unlike a Researched Argument Paper, which requires you to develop an argumentative thesis, about which reasonable people might disagree, and support that thesis, and that thesis alone, in the body of your paper, a Research Paper asks you to inform yourself and your audience more broadly about the topic.

For this assignment, you will read several primary and secondary sources on your topic. Then, you will share your newly found knowledge in the form of a research paper, integrating scholarly sources into your paper using summary, paraphrase, and quotation. You will need to choose an organization that supports your readers' likely expertise regarding the topic, recognizing that your readers, the A-State University community, are bright and know a lot about many things, but they don't know everything. To this end, you may need to provide background information, identify important concepts and people, and define key terms.

Sample Essay in Chicago Style

William Kazyak

Written for Marcus Tribbett's Composition II Class

· ·

· ·

Note: As you will see, William's essay has been formatted into Chicago style. As is customary in Chicago style, William has included footnotes and a bibliography.

· ·

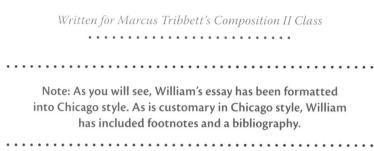

Deception and Destruction: Operation Fortitude and the Allied Aerial Support for Operation Overlord

William Kazyak

Composition II

Professor Tribbett

March 29, 2014

1

"We're going in alone, and I don't think we're coming back" rang the words of Wing Commander Josef "Pips" Priller to his wingman, Sergeant Heinz Wodarczyk, on June 6, 1944 with the bleak prospect of their mission. They were embarking on a mission to disrupt, as far as they could, the massive Allied landings on the Normandy beaches. They would be flying into an area infested with hostile aircraft and anti-aircraft guns that would surely shoot them out of the sky before they had a chance to mount an attack. However, Priller and his wingman did make one pass on Sword Beach.[1] It was the only attack made by the German Luftwaffe (air force) on that historic day.[2] The reasons for this have become clear over the decades since D-Day. By June 6, 1944, the Allies had whittled the Luftwaffe down to a mere shadow of its early war glory and gained complete superiority in the skies over Europe.

Air superiority itself, however, did not ensure the success of Operation Overlord. At this point, even without air superiority, the Germans possessed the means for a successful counterattack that could dislodge the allies and throw them back into the sea. The reasons for their lack of appropriate reaction to the invasion stemmed primarily from the fact that the Allies had deceived them concerning the date, location, and force of the invasion through a series of elaborate and ingenious ruses. Code named Operation Fortitude, these efforts, in conjunction with aerial dominance by the Allies, provided critical support to Operation Overlord.

Operation Fortitude was officially put into action on February 23, 1944; less than four months prior to the date of the Overlord landings.[3] Anthony Cave Brown, in his book *Bodyguard of Lies*, gives a very direct and comprehensive statement of the goals of Fortitude. Fortitude was designed to: 1) cause the Germans to make strategic errors by threatening Norway,

---

1. Wynn, *Prelude to Overlord*, 138.

2. McFarland, "Air Combat," 11.

3. Hinsley, "Deception," 174.

2) mislead them concerning the location and date of Overlord, and 3) cause them to make poor strategic decisions after the landings by threatening the Pas de Calais region of France.[4]

The first goal of Operation Fortitude was accomplished by one of its two distinct operations, Fortitude North. Norway was a valuable strategic asset for Germany because it was one of their primary naval bases.[5] Germany had a total of twenty-seven divisions of soldiers stationed in Northwest Europe (including Norway) to guard against an attack there.[6] These soldiers, had they been allowed to be used to reinforce France, could have caused major problems for Overlord, so the Allies had to find a way to keep them in Northwest Europe. Fortunately, Adolf Hitler himself was obsessed with Norway as an asset and was determined to keep it at all costs.[7] This made it relatively easy for the planners of Fortitude North to figure out how to pin down German forces in Norway. In conjunction with the Soviets, the Allies devised a plan to assemble a fake army in Scotland, thereby threatening a two-front invasion. Brown relates the assembly of this army in great detail. In Scotland, the Allies utilized a number of ingenious methods to simulate the build-up of forces of what was supposed to be the British 4th Army Group. The primary method used was bogus radio traffic. A few skilled radio units could move around broadcasting messages to each other that sounded exactly like communications between different units of an army group. This was supplemented by calculated leaks to newspapers, radio, and other press about events supposedly going on involving units in the 4th army. Other methods included placing ships and dummy aircraft in plain view of German recon planes, as well as the purchase of £500,000 of Scandinavian securities by the British; actions that were interpreted by the Germans to mean that an invasion of Northwest Europe was

---

4. Brown, *Bodyguard of Lies*, 460.

5. Penrose, *The D-Day Companion*, 61.

6. Brown, *Bodyguard of Lies*, 460.

7. Ibid., 462.

3

imminent. But the icing on the cake came from agents of Britain's then-secret "XX-Committee," or Double Cross System. XX's agents "Mutt" and "Jeff" both played key roles in Fortitude North by feeding the Germans a mix of false and true information. One of their reports was that Soviet intelligence officer Klementi Budyenny had come to England to discuss the joint invasion of Norway. In reality, Budyenny did come to England, but only to discuss the role the Russians were to play in Fortitude.[8]

Fortitude South was implemented in much the same way as Fortitude North, only it was more involved and played on more of the Germans' pre-dispositions. In the first place, Fortitude South directly threatened an invasion in the Pas de Calais region of France.[9] This part of France was separated from England (specifically Dover) by a mere 25 miles of water.[10] This was the shortest distance between France and England, and the Germans knew this as well as the Allies. The Germans, for their part, built up their strength here, and even stationed the 15th Army, their best soldiers on the Western Front, at Calais.[11] The Allies, for their part, were determined to see to it that those defenses stayed in Calais and were not redeployed to Normandy; at least not until a significant and irreversible build up had occurred.[12] Here again, the Allies turned to bogus armies for this effort. They built-up FUSAG, the First U. S. Army Group, around the command of Lt. General George S. Patton, Jr., an American whom the Germans considered the best Allied commander and expected to lead the invasion.[13] The assembly of FUSAG utilized essentially the same methods as the assembly of 4th Army. Dummy ships, aircraft, tanks and installations as well as calculated press releases and skilled radio operators transmitting build-up

---

8. Brown, *Bodyguard of Lies*, 464–68.

9. Hinsley, "Deception," 174.

10. Drez, *Voices of D-Day*, 19.

11. Brown, *Bodyguard of Lies*, 461.

12. Penrose, *The D-Day Companion*, 56.

13. Ibid.; Ambrose, "Eisenhower," 267.

4

communications all contributed to the FUSAG scam, and as with the 4th Army deception, XX's agents added further to the confusion. The agents code-named "Garbo" (who was the Germans' most trusted agent) and "Tricycle" played important parts in the scheme, primarily by feeding false information to the Germans.[14]

Fortitude South had one more key aspect: aerial deception. Prior to D-Day, the Allies implemented a strategy to disable as much of the German war effort as possible. This included coastal defenses, airfields, and rail targets.[15] However, if they bombed one area more heavily than the other, the Germans may have deduced the location of the invasion from that strategy. The Allies, therefore, proceeded to attack targets in Calais twice as hard as targets in Normandy in an extension of the effort to make the Germans look to Calais for the invasion.[16] A second role that aircraft played in Fortitude came in a revolutionary new area of warfare: electronic countermeasures. By D-Day, the Allies had developed radar-jamming devices like Window, Moonshine, and Filberts, and had discovered that when properly used in conjunction, they would paint a picture on radar screens of an invasion fleet headed in a certain direction. These methods were perfected and put into practice for D-Day.[17]

The Allies had obviously taken great pains to conceal their true intentions concerning Overlord; now the question was whether or not the Germans would take the bait. *The D-Day Companion*, edited by Jane Penrose, states that Fortitude did not cause the Germans to alter their battle plans; however, this statement is misleading on the surface.[18] According to Brown, the Germans actually reinforced their Norwegian garrisons.[19]

---

14. Brown, *Bodyguard of Lies*, 480–89.

15. Ibid., 521.

16. Penrose, *The D-Day Companion*, 62.

17. Brown, *Bodyguard of Lies*, 524–26.

18. Penrose, *The D-Day Companion*, 63.

19. Brown, *Bodyguard of Lies*, 472.

5

Nevertheless, little response to Fortitude was observed prior to D-Day. It was only after the landings that the staggering success of this astronomical effort was felt. The Germans hesitated to reinforce Normandy for as long as two weeks.[20] Thanks to reports from "Garbo" that Normandy was a fake and FUSAG still planned to invade Calais, the Germans not only failed to reinforce Normandy, but they recalled two Panzer divisions and an infantry division that were already en-route to Normandy and sent them to Calais.[21] The inflated order of battle that "Tricycle" had given the Germans prior to D-Day also came into play by conning the Germans into thinking that most of the Allies' forces were still in England waiting to pounce on Calais the minute they withdrew any forces from there.[22] Overall, Fortitude kept the Germans groping in the dark for the Allies' real intentions until the middle of July, and by that time Allied forces had built-up to the point where it would have been difficult at best to dislodge them.[23]

While this battle of wits was raging, another crucial battle was erupting in the skies over Europe as a prerequisite to D-Day. This was the battle for air superiority. Air superiority had been a major factor in another planned amphibious invasion earlier in the war: Operation Sea Lion, the German plan to invade England.[24] The Germans, however, had not been able to wrest control of the skies over Southern England and the English Channel from the British Royal Air Force, and now they were facing the same challenges that the RAF had met four years earlier. Both the Allies and the Germans knew how crucial air superiority was, and both fought tenaciously for it.

---

20. Budiansky, "The Art of the Double Cross," 44.

21. Ibid.

22. Brown, *Bodyguard of Lies*, 487–99.

23. Penrose, *The D-Day Companion*, 64.

24. Galland, "The First and the Last," 10–16.

Dwight D. Eisenhower, the Supreme Allied Commander, had promised his troops prior to D-Day that, "if you see fighting aircraft over you, they will be ours."[25] This bold promise was not an empty one. Since 1943, Allied Bomber crews had been waging a costly war of attrition with the Germans in their attempts to knock out German industry.[26] The arrival of long-range fighter escorts (in particular the P-51 Mustang, which was superior to the German aircraft in nearly every aspect) changed the war entirely.[27] Now it was the Germans who were suffering catastrophic losses, in terms of both pilots and aircraft. At the beginning of 1944, the Germans had 2,395 fighter pilots available for combat, with about half of them actually ready to engage in battle. By the middle of the year, ninety-nine percent of these pilots had been lost.[28] Their aircraft strength had hardly fared better. By D-Day, only forty percent of their total available aircraft (on all fronts) were operable, and on top of that they had pulled the majority of their fighters back to Germany.[29] The German Third Air Force in France was left with around 100 fighters to stop an Allied onslaught of 6,000–7,000 bombers and fighters.[30] Even when the Germans did order their fighters in Germany to head to France, P-51 patrols intercepted and shot down between thirty and fifty percent of them.[31] Those that escaped the dogfights often crashed before reaching their bases due to poor cross country training of the pilots.[32] Fourteen days after the start of the invasion, the German fighter reinforcements were no longer able to fight and were pulled back to Germany.[33]

---

25. McFarland, "Air Combat," 12.

26. Wynn, *Prelude to Overlord*, 14.

27. Penrose, *The D-Day Companion*, 118.

28. Ibid., 120–21.

29. Galland, *The First and the Last*, 211; Penrose, *The D-Day Companion*, 117.

30. Galland, *The First and the Last*, 213.

31. McFarland, "Air Combat," 11.

32. Galland, *The First and the Last*, 215.

33. Ibid., 219.

While Allied long-range fighters systematically decimated the Luftwaffe, Allied bombers and fighter-bombers were waging an important tactical war to destroy the Germans' ability to reinforce Normandy. The primary aspect of this battle, known as the Transportation Plan, was aimed at obliterating the French Railway system. The Germans relied heavily on this system for movement of troops and especially armored vehicles, such as tanks.[34] Beginning in March, 1944, the Allies pulverized thirty-six rail yards with no less than 139 raids. After May 20, 1944, the juggernaut of the Allied air forces was unleashed against railway bridges and even individual trains. By D-Day, every bridge over the Seine River from Conflans to Rouen, a total of no less than thirty-five crossings, had been reduced to chunks of concrete and steel protruding from the water.[35]

The Transportation Plan effectively neutralized the Germans' ability to reinforce Normandy. The Allies had successfully disabled the Germans' quickest and most effective means of supply and reinforcement. Panzer divisions trying to get to Normandy, now forced to travel under their own power, took anywhere from five days to three weeks to arrive in the battle zone. Even then, their transit was turned into a nightmare as Allied fighter-bombers destroyed anything that moved (tanks were especially prime targets).[36]

On D-Day itself, the Allies made sure that the air over the fleet and the beaches was well covered. During the daytime, P-38 Lightning fighters guarded the shipping lanes between France and England, and when night arrived, the RAF took over the task with a force of night fighters. The beaches were covered by RAF Spitfire fighters down low and by USAAF P-47 Thunderbolt fighters up high. The Allies even added an extra insurance to the landings by sending P-51 Mustangs and more P-38s to form a kill zone

---

34. Ambrose, "Eisenhower," 270.

35. Wynn, *Prelude to Overlord*, 104–6.

36. Penrose, *The D-Day Companion*, 123.

further inland with the aim of stopping any German planes long before they got to the beaches. P-47s and RAF Typhoon fighter-bombers provided close support to the troops by hitting tanks and other vehicles and by neutralizing threats when called upon by the ground forces. Only two Luftwaffe aircraft (the Fw-190 fighters flown by Priller and Wodarczyk) got through to the Allied landing zone; a stunning fulfillment of Eisenhower's promise.[37]

On July 31, 1944, the Allies broke out of Saint-Lô, France, making Overlord an official success.[38] This success, though, came about largely due to the cunning of Allied intelligence officers and the skill and bravery of Allied airmen. Operation Fortitude's stunning success in pinning down German forces elsewhere in Europe and in delaying orders to reinforce Normandy played a major role in buying the Allies the precious time they needed to consolidate their foothold in Europe, and Allied air power supplemented this by destroying both the Luftwaffe and the Germans' means of transportation. Looking back on Overlord, Eisenhower stated that "Without the overwhelming mastery of the air which we attained by that time, our assault on the Continent would have been a most hazardous, if not impossible undertaking," and Adolf Galland, the German Fighter Commander at the time of the invasion, echoes this statement in his book *The First and the Last*.[39] When Priller and Wodarczyk returned to their base after their bold attack on Sword beach, the best they could really do was sit back and look helplessly on as the Third Reich began to crumble under the massive Allied juggernaut; a juggernaut enabled and supported by a brilliant combination of deception and destruction.

---

37. Wynn, *Prelude to Overlord*, 137–38.

38. Galland, *The First and the Last*, 225.

39. Wynn, *Prelude to Overlord*, 26; Galland, *The First and the Last*, 225.

9

Bibliography

Ambrose, Stephen E. "Eisenhower, the Intelligence Community, and the D-Day Invasion." *The Wisconsin Magazine of History* 64, no. 4 (1981): 261–77.

Brown, Anthony Cave. *Bodyguard of Lies*. New York: Harper and Row, Publishers, Inc., 1975.

Budiansky, Stephen. "The Art of the Double Cross." *World War II*, 24, no. 1 (2009): 38–45.

Drez, Ronald J., ed. *Voices of D-Day*. Baton Rouge: Louisiana State University Press, 1994.

Galland, Adolf. *The First and the Last: The Rise and Fall of the German Fighter Forces, 1938–1945*, 2nd ed. Translated by Mervyn Savill. Cutchogue, NY: Buccaneer Books, 1954.

Hinsley, F. H. "Deception." *The D-Day Encyclopedia*. 1994.

McFarland, Stephen L. "Air Combat." *The D-Day Encyclopedia*. 1994.

Penrose, Jane, ed. *The D-Day Companion*. Oxford, United Kingdom: Osprey Publishing, 2004.

Ryan, Cornelius. *The Longest Day: June 6, 1944*. New York: Simon and Schuster, 1959.

Wynn, Humphrey and Susan Young. *Prelude to Overlord: An Account of the Air Operations Which Preceded and Supported Operation Overlord, the Allied Landings in Normandy on D-Day, 6th of June 1944*. Novato, CA: Presidio Press, 1984.

Photo courtesy of William Kazyak

COURTNEY BAKER

Courtney Baker is an avid outdoors-person hailing from Yellville, AR. Courtney enjoys hunting, fishing, kayaking, and camping. She carries this enjoyment of nature into her major in Agricultural Business.

Courtney finds that arranging her thoughts is easier in writing than in speaking. She utilizes an outlining and peer-review process when writing for an assignment. Courtney says that once an outline is in place for a work, "putting it into essay or short-story form is a breeze." When asked specifically about her piece, "Coal Mining: From Providing to Destroying," she credits peer-revision with assisting in finalizing the essay printed here.

Courtney urges her fellow students to have their work reviewed by others. Her initial skepticism of visiting a writing tutor was assuaged when she realized that the tutor helped her "see gaps" in her writing that she "never would have recognized" on her own.

THE ASSIGNMENT: OP-ED

Opposite Editorials or Op-Eds are short, journalistic, argument-driven pieces commonly found in newspapers and online publications. Op-Eds can focus on almost anything: cultural, political, social, humanitarian, educational, or financial issues; particular people, places, or events; or even, another Op-Ed. While informative, an Op-Ed's main purpose is to persuade the reader to see the issue, event, person, or place as the writer does. In fact, some Op-Eds go a step further and, in addition to adding to the readers' previous understanding of the issue, ask for the readers to take action, such as writing a congresswoman a letter or boycotting a restaurant because of its discriminatory practices.

For this assignment, you will write an Op-Ed on a contemporary issue of interest to you. As you begin your paper, consider: what sources and perspectives are missing from the current conversations and media coverage of this topic; what sources, information, and perspectives will add ethos to your argument; and what voice you, the writer, should adopt to best persuade your readers. Keep in mind that the tone and style of an Op-Ed should be dependent on its content, purpose, and audience. Many Op-Eds adopt informal, conversational tones and utilize colloquialisms.

Sample Essay in APA Style

Courtney Baker

Written for Marcus Tribbett's Composition II Class

· ·

· ·

Note: As you will see, Courtney's essay has been formatted into APA style. As is customary in APA style, Courtney has not included signal phrases throughout her piece where she has integrated sources. Instead, she has included only the in-text citation.

· ·

Running head: COAL MINING   1

Coal Mining: From Providing to Destroying

Courtney Baker

Arkansas State University

COAL MINING   2

Coal Mining: From Providing to Destroying

Coal mining in the Appalachian Mountains of West Virginia seems as natural as the abundant forest that covers the land. For many years these hills have provided the United States with its primary source of electricity—coal. Recently, however, tides have changed in the coal mining industry, bringing a new method of mining that is leaving West Virginians in a heated debate. It is called Mountaintop Removal Valley-Fill Mining (MRVF). This process involves blowing the top off of a mountain using dynamite and then "stripping" the seams of coal that lay exposed after the blast (Geller, 2009). The efficiency of this act has been out-weighed by its perceived stigma, and the controversy that surrounds it sees no end in sight. Ultimately, as is revealed in the informative documentary *Coal Country*, MRVF is the center point in an argument that is less about the method and more about money, beliefs, and long-standing ways of life (Geller, 2009).

One of the initial rationales for developing MRVF was its potential to save money. As opposed to underground mining, surface mining does not require near as many workers (Geller, 2009). Therefore, the mining companies are obligated to pay far fewer employees, which is where the companies see the bulk of their savings. Additionally, without the use of underground mining tunnels, there are far fewer safety precautions that must be met. Being able to extract coal without having to build safe tunneling for employees allows companies to cut safety costs and ship out coal even quicker than before. Thus, MRVF is less costly and more efficient, which leads directly to increased profit.

The question remains though, if MRVF is so cheap and efficient, why isn't it the universally preferred mining method? This is because while MRVF is profitable for the mining companies, it has not been profitable for the workers. This is illustrated through the mining district in West Virginia, which is no longer seeing profit from its rich resources. The money being made from the region's coal is being monopolized strictly within the mining companies (Geller, 2009). Because of this, communities in the mining hills are quickly fading, many workers have lost their jobs, and many of the towns are now ghost towns with only a few faithful citizens. These once-thriving mining communities provide the majority of our country's electricity, yet the people that live there are now struggling to get by while the mining companies are making record profits.

Further opposition to MRVF comes from those who find that it conflicts with their values such as conservationists. Conservationists are leading contenders in the fight against surface mining because it destroys so much of the Appalachian mountain range. When the miners remove the mountaintops, the mountains are gone forever. Proponents of MRVF, such as the mining companies who utilize this method, argue that they "reclaim" the mountain after they are done. This involves spreading the discarded rock back along the mining site to resurface the location as best they can (Geller, 2009). This may technically be true, but these reclamation sites are easily distinguished from the rest of the forest because they do not allow for comparable diverse vegetative growth. Environmental advocates are fighting for the preservation of the mountains and the forests that thrive on them. The miners and the mining companies, however, see it a little differently, believing that, as long as the mountain is there and the coal is inside, they have the right to harvest it and use it to their benefit.

Somewhere in the middle of this debate are the coal miners, many of who want to mine the way they always have, the way their fathers did, and the way their fathers' fathers did. They argue that mining has been a way of life for hundreds of years and that without coal mining, the communities present in places like Appalachia, West Virginia will be literally nonexistent.

COAL MINING   4

In the end, MRVF is more efficient and less costly for the coal mining companies, but at what cost to the mining communities and the environment? The costs to coal miners, citizens of mining districts, and the environment are grave and many. By cutting jobs, and destroying and polluting the land, MRVF and the coal mining companies are not helping preserve coal mining heritage or the environment, they are destroying them, and, ultimately, only helping themselves.

Reference

Geller, P. (Director & Producer). (2009). *Coal Country* [Motion picture]. United States: Evening Star Productions.

Library and Information Research

Robert Robinette

Student Success Librarian at Arkansas State University

· ·

"I don't use the library. I never need it."

—Bertha Bumpkin, sophomore Bellybutton Studies major

This type of comment frustrates librarians, but it has some truth to it. You can hop on Google, misspell a few words, and instantly have millions of results on any topic imaginable. The problem, of course, is that much of what you find is worthless. We are inundated with "fake news," propaganda, disguised advertisements, infotainment, and other misleading or inaccurate sources. In a 2016 Stanford University study, more than 80% of students were unable to identify a story prominently labeled "sponsored content" as an advertisement (Stanford 10). Surrounded by constant social media updates, app notifications, and a 24-hour news cycle, students often fail to take advantage of the library's invaluable research tools and quality information sources. Thus, in this section, you will learn about trustworthy, high-quality information sources available to you through the library.

Scholarly Sources

You will hear the term *scholarly* a lot in college, usually in the context of *scholarly journals*, also known as *academic*, *peer-reviewed*, or *refereed* journals. Scholarly journals contain articles written by expert scholars (usually somebody with an advanced degree in the field) for other expert scholars. These articles almost always undergo peer-review, i.e., they are chosen for publication by other experts in the discipline.[1] They also provide extensive documentation of their sources, i.e., they have a bibliography listing their sources. Along with these key features, scholarly journals typically have one goal in mind: contributing new knowledge to a discipline. Scholarly

---

1 A discipline is another term for a field of study, e.g., Biology or Political Science.

sources may possess other attributes—for instance, they might use technical language or jargon, assume you have background knowledge of the topic, or use discipline-specific research methods—but these will vary from discipline to discipline. You can find scholarly journal articles and other quality sources by searching the library's many research databases.

Research Databases

The A-State library subscribes to hundreds of **research databases** that provide access to thousands of information sources, including scholarly journals, e-books, government documents, research reports, and more. Research databases come in a few primary types:

- *General databases*, such as **JSTOR**, provide sources from a wide variety of disciplines in a wide variety of formats.

- *Specialized databases* focus on a specific discipline or set of disciplines. For example, **ABI/Inform** focuses exclusively on Business sources.

- *Aggregated databases* such as **OneSearch** and **ProQuest Central** are very large databases that collect several databases into one searchable interface. These are often the best places to begin your research because you can almost always find something on even the most esoteric topic.

Most information research will require you to search several databases, so if you do not find what you need in one database, try another—we have plenty.

If you use the library, you will never have to pay for access to information! Even if we do not immediately have access to something you need, we can request it from another library for free by using a service called *Interlibrary Loan.*

For some assignments and projects, professors might require *primary sources*, which are information sources without any layer of analysis or interpretation over them. A *secondary source* comments on, critiques, or otherwise analyzes a primary source. In history and other humanities disciplines, primary sources refer to information sources from the time being studied, e.g., a firsthand account of an earthquake. In the sciences, primary sources typically refer to original research articles, e.g., a report on a study of mutant barnacles. Where you search for primary sources will depend on the discipline in question and your research needs. You might use the **library's primary resources databases** or the **library catalog**, which is the searchable interface for everything the library owns. You might even need to dig a little deeper and use the **university archives**, which is where we store and preserve rare and fragile research materials.

Conducting Effective Searches

Knowing how to access quality library sources is great, but if you struggle to formulate an effective search, you will never find what you need. Here are some quick tips to improve your searches:

* *Search, search, and search again*: Your first few searches will probably be clumsy and demonstrate your lack of knowledge. As you find new sources and learn more about your topic, you will discover new terms to use and new avenues of research to explore. Trying a different search strategy never hurts.

* *Be specific, but not too specific*: Searching for *medical marijuana* is too broad. Searching for *medical marijuana Arkansas children autism garbanzo beans* is probably too specific. You must strike the right balance.

* *Use Boolean search operators*: The *OR* operator will expand your search (useful for synonyms, e.g., *medical marijuana OR medical cannabis*), the *AND* operator will narrow your search, and the *NOT* operator will exclude certain terms. An effective search commonly uses a combination of Boolean operators.

* *Search for specific phrases*: Most databases will allow you to search for a specific phrase by placing it in quotation marks. For example, *"medical marijuana"* retrieves results with that exact phrase whereas *medical marijuana* might give you results on medical devices and growing marijuana but nothing about the concept of "medical marijuana."

* *Use search limits*: You often find too much information. When this happens, it can be helpful to set search limits. You might set a limit for a specific date range, material type, language, or discipline. Setting limits generally provides a more manageable set of results.

Sometimes you search and search and search to no avail. If you struggle to find what you need, **contact a librarian** to help get you on the right track.

The Physical Library

As an undergraduate, you can check out up to twenty of the hundreds of thousands of books, films, government documents, maps, games, and other sources in the library, all of which can be located via the **library catalog**. In addition, the library contains:

* Dozens of computers located throughout the library;

* Several printers to use for free printing;

* 23 study rooms, many with whiteboards (you can check out markers from the service desk);

- A presentation room with a projector;
- Innumerable nooks and crannies to hole up in;
- Librarians and library staff ~~with sweet dance moves~~ who can help you with your research.

The library is a welcoming, inviting place with an atmosphere highly conducive to research and creativity. We hope to see you around.

Want to make your mark at 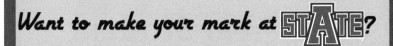?

Want the chance to win cash prizes?

Submit your best
Comp I and II paper to

Pack Prints

Submissions may be sent to:

$100 awarded
to top paper!
Additional cash prizes
will be awarded to
selected works.

packprintsasu@gmail.com

Be sure to attach
your paper in a Word Doc.
Also include your full name,
the course, and the assignment
for which the paper was written
in the body of your email.

Please direct questions to:
Kristi Costello
kcostello@astate.edu

First-Year Student Survival Contact List

Brought to you by the Arkansas State University Writing Center Tutors

ADMISSIONS

Location: 2nd Floor Student Union, rm. 2130 • **Phone Number**: 870-972-2031

Purpose: You got in. Isn't that enough?! Not necessarily. The Admissions Office can assist you with the gamut of Admission questions.

CAREER SERVICES

Location: 2nd Floor Student Union, rm. 2167 • **Phone Number**: 870-972-3025

Purpose: Do you know what you want to be when you grow up? Do you need help making that dream a reality? Career Services can help you on both accounts! They provide career services and programs for students attending school in the A-State system, including help with job placement and resumes.

COUNSELING CENTER

Location: 2nd Floor Student Union, rm. 2203 • **Phone Number**: 870-972-2318

Purpose: Have an issue? Need a tissue? Counseling is available for free for all A-State students. Walk-in appointments may be available, but cannot be guaranteed. Walk-in hours are Monday–Thursday 12:00 pm–3:00 pm and Friday 9:00 am–noon.

DINING SERVICES

Location: 2nd Floor Student Union, rm. 2064 B • **Phone Number**: 870-972-2059

Purpose: Are you hungry like the wolf? Dining Services can answer questions regarding food and catering as well as offer job opportunities.

DISABILITY SERVICES

Location: 2nd Floor Student Union, rm. 2181 • **Phone Number**: 870-972-3964

Purpose: Disability Services focuses on facilitating opportunities to stimulate and create a barrier free environment eliminating academic, social, and physical obstacles which impede students' access to a higher education.

FINANCIAL AID

Location: 2nd Floor Student Union, rm. 2078 • **Phone Number**: 870-972-2310

Purpose: "Money, money, money moneeey!" This office can assist you by providing guidance through the financial aid process.

GAY-STRAIGHT ALLIANCE (GSA)

Contact: Joy Mayall

Purpose: The purpose of the Gay-Straight Alliance is to help students and faculty understand the lesbian, gay, bisexual and transgendered community. Activities include workshops, weekly meetings, special events, and other educational activities to help build a safer and more tolerant environment for all LGBTQIA students and their allies at Arkansas State University.

HEALTH CENTER

Location: 333B Red Wolf Blvd. • **Phone Number**: 870-972-2054

Purpose: You can visit the health center for treatment of minor illnesses and injuries, physical exams, immunizations, PAP smears, STI testing, and prescription medications. Students may be referred to other facilities for additional laboratory tests, X-rays, diagnostic imaging, counseling, or specialized services.

Additional Resources

HONORS COLLEGE

Location: 1st Floor Library, rm. 103 • **Phone Number**: 870-972-2308

Purpose: The Honors Office supports Honors students in their academic pursuits and brings them together for trips, social and community events, and service-learning opportunities.

LEADERSHIP CENTER

Location: 2nd Floor Student Union • **Phone Number**: 870-972-2055

Purpose: The Leadership Center offers programs and services that foster leadership development through community service, encouraging the creation of lasting connections and the recognition of accomplishments.

LEARNING COMMONS

Location: Dean B. Ellis Library (Downstairs), rm. 133 •
Phone Number: 870-972-3451

Purpose: You can visit the Learning Commons for drop-in peer, one-on-one, and small-group tutoring in almost all ASU-J 1000- and 2000-level general education courses as well as some upper-division core courses.

MULTICULTURAL CENTER

Location: 3rd Floor Student Union, rm. 3003 • **Director**: Evette Allen
Phone Number: 870-680-4052

Purpose: Established in 2010, the Multicultural Center (MC) strives to sustain an inclusive campus environment that values and respects ALL members of the university community.

NON-TRADITIONAL STUDENT OFFICE

Location: 3rd Floor Library, rm. 3003 • **Phone Number**: 870-972-4052

Purpose: The purpose of NTSO is to advocate and support the success of non-traditional students at A-State.

PARKING SERVICES

Location: 2301D E. Johnson Dr. • **Phone Number**: 870-972-2945

Purpose: This is where you go to get your parking sticker and to get information about fighting those pesky tickets. Remember to renew your sticker every fall!

RED WOLF CENTER

Location: Red Wolf Center, rm. 104, 2505 Aggie Road • **Phone Number**: 870-972-3800

Purpose: The Red Wolf Center is a recreational and exercise facility open and free to all A-State students who yearn to shed those pesky extra pounds, simply be healthier, or just have some fun.

RESIDENCE LIFE

Location: 2nd Floor Student Union, rm. 2053 • **Phone Number**: 870-972-2042

Purpose: Residence Life provides a safe, diverse, and well-maintained environment that complements and supports the academic mission of the University. If students have questions or concerns about their on-campus living situations, they should contact Residence Life.

STUDENT ACCOUNTS

Location: 2nd Floor Student Union, rm. 2146 • **Phone Number**: 870-972-2285

Purpose: The Office of Student Accounts is the centralized billing and collection point for student accounts. The primary function of the office is to issue bills, receive payments and provide information to help students understand the aspects of their account.

STUDENT GOVERNMENT ASSOCIATION

Contact: Hannah Aldridge • **Advisor**: Martha Spack

Purpose: The Student Government Association serves as the official voice of the student body.

STUDENT PHILANTHROPY COUNCIL

Contact: Jessica Blackburn • **Phone Number**: 870-972-2060

Purpose: The SPC strives to support the mission and purpose of A-State by providing a student perspective on giving, promoting awareness of the ways private gifts impact student life, and establishing a culture of philanthropy that enhances the future of Arkansas State University.

TESTING CENTER

Location: 3rd Floor Student Union, rm. 3034 • **Phone Number**: 870-972-2038

Purpose: The A-State Testing Center is certified by Educational Testing Service (ETS), American College Testing (ACT), The College Board, Pearson VUE and several private boards and societies to efficiently coordinate the organization, administration, and security of 18 different standardized testing programs.

VOLUNTEER A-STATE

Contact: Emilee Taylor

Purpose: Want to get served by serving others? Volunteer A-State provides the Arkansas State University student body a place to serve, learn, and #makeastAtement by partnering with nonprofits and promoting social justice.

WRITING CENTER

Location: Dean B. Ellis Library (Downstairs), rm. 133 • **Phone Number**: 870-972-3451

Purpose: The A-State Writing Center strives to make better writers, not just better writing. We will help ALL students on ANY assignment at ANY stage of the writing process for ANY course. We are a valuable resource for students who feel overwhelmed with writing assignments or writing, in general, as well as a great place for seasoned writers to get additional eyes on their papers.

Enjoy Writing?
Why Not Declare a Minor in Writing Studies?

The new Writing Studies minor has three tracks: General Writing Studies, Creative Writing, and Professional Writing.

Which will you choose?

Required Courses* (General Track)	
BSE English students may substitute EDEN 4553, Methods and Materials for Teaching English for the Preceptorship and Internship. BSE English students may also substitute ENG 4043, Theory in the Teaching of Composition, as one of their Writing Studies Electives. THEA 4313 and CMP 3403 cannot be used by students majoring in the College of Media & Communication to fulfill this minor. Creative Writing courses may be repeated with various topics.	Sem. Hrs.
ENG 3033, Introduction to Writing Studies	3
ENG 4711, Preceptorship in Writing Studies	1
ENG 4722, Internship in Writing Studies	2
Elective from Professional Writing Track (ENG 3003, ENG 3013, ENG 3043, ENG 4703, or ENG 3053)	3
Elective from Creative Writing Track (ENG 3023, ENG 4023, THEA 4313, or CMP 3403)	3
Electives in Writing Studies	6
Total Required Hours:	**18**
Required Courses (Creative Writing Track) See above for possible substitutions.	Sem. Hrs.
ENG 3033, Introduction to Writing Studies	3
ENG 3023, Creative Writing, and/or ENG 4023, Advanced Creative Writing (Courses may be repeated with various topics; may also include either THEA 4313, Fundamentals of Playwriting, or CMP 4303, Screenwriting for Narrative Motion Pictures)	9
ENG 4711, Preceptorship in Writing Studies	1
ENG 4722, Internship in Writing Studies	2
Electives in Writing Studies	3
Total Required Hours:	**18**

Required Courses (Professional Writing Track) See above for possible substitutions.	Sem. Hrs.
ENG 3003, Advanced Composition	3
ENG 3013, Practical Writing	3
ENG 3033, Introduction to Writing Studies	3
ENG 3043, Technical Writing	3
ENG 4711, Preceptorship in Writing Studies	1
ENG 4722, Internship in Writing Studies	2
Electives in Writing Studies	3
Total Required Hours:	**18**

If you have questions about the Writing Studies Minor, contact Dr. Kristi Costello at kcostello@astate.edu or visit the Department of English and Philosophy.

* Obtained from the Campus Writing Program's website at **http://www.astate.edu/ college/liberal-arts/departments/english-and-philosophy/writing-guide/writing- studies/writing-studies-minor/**.

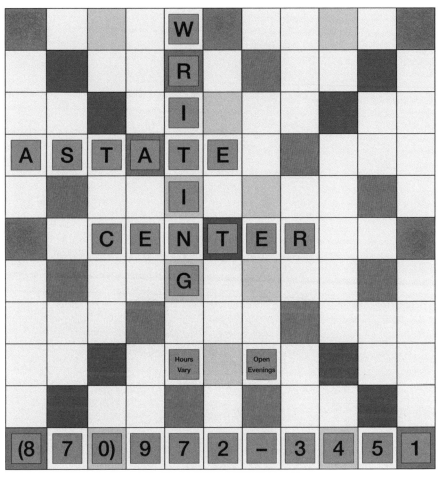

The Writing Center is located on the first floor of the
Dean B. Ellis Library.

We work with ALL students on ANY assignment at ANY stage of the
writing process.

Now offering Skype Appointments!

Call to make an appointment or drop in during business hours.

If you have any questions about our services, please contact the
Director of the Writing Program and Writing Center,
Dr. Kristi Costello at kcostello@astate.edu.